N1998.3.L434

owning, Lisa

atrice Lecor

2004.

| DATE DUE | RETURNED |
|----------|----------|
|          |          |
|          |          |
|          |          |
|          |          |
|          |          |
|          |          |
|          |          |
|          |          |
|          |          |
|          |          |
|          |          |
|          |          |
|          |          |
|          |          |
|          |          |
|          |          |

# Patrice Leconte

Published in our
centenary year
~ **2004** ~
MANCHESTER
UNIVERSITY
PRESS

FRENCH FILM DIRECTORS

DIANA HOLMES and ROBERT INGRAM *series editors*
DUDLEY ANDREW *series consultant*

**Jean-Jacques Beineix**   PHIL POWRIE

**Luc Besson**   SUSAN HAYWARD

**Bertrand Blier**   SUE HARRIS

**Robert Bresson**   KEITH READER

**Leos Carax**   GARIN DOWD AND FERGUS DALEY

**Claude Chabrol**   GUY AUSTIN

**Claire Denis**   MARTINE BEUGNET

**Marguerite Duras**   RENATE GÜNTHER

**Diane Kurys**   CARRIE TARR

**Louis Malle**   HUGO FREY

**Georges Méliès**   ELIZABETH EZRA

**Jean Renoir**   MARTIN O'SHAUGHNESSY

**Coline Serreau**   BRIGITTE ROLLET

**François Truffaut**   DIANA HOLMES AND ROBERT INGRAM

**Agnès Varda**   ALISON SMITH

FRENCH FILM DIRECTORS

# Patrice Leconte

LISA DOWNING

*165101*

**Manchester University Press**
MANCHESTER AND NEW YORK

distributed exclusively in the USA by Palgrave

The right of Lisa Downing to be identified as the author of this work
has been asserted by her in accordance with the Copyright,
Designs and Patents Act 1988.

*Published by* Manchester University Press
Oxford Road, Manchester M13 9NR, UK
*and* Room 400, 175 Fifth Avenue, New York, NY 10010, USA
www.manchesteruniversitypress.co.uk

*Distributed exclusively in the USA by*
Palgrave, 175 Fifth Avenue, New York, NY 10010, USA

*Distributed exclusively in Canada by*
UBC Press, University of British Columbia, 2029 West Mall, Vancouver,
BC, Canada V6T 1Z2

*British Library Cataloguing-in-Publication Data*
A catalogue record for this book is available from the British Library

*Library of Congress Cataloging-in-Publication Data applied for*

ISBN 0 7190 6424 4 *hardback*
EAN 978 0 7190 6424 1
ISBN 0 7190 6425 2 *paperback*
EAN 978 0 7190 6425 8

First published 2004

12 11 10 09 08 07 06 05 04     10 9 8 7 6 5 4 3 2 1

Typeset in Scala with Meta display
by Koinonia, Manchester
Printed in Great Britain
by Biddles Ltd, King's Lynn

# Contents

# List of plates

Figures 2, 10, 11 and 12 are reproduced by permission of Catherine Cabrol. Figures 3 and 5 are reproduced by permission of Jean-Marie Leroy. Every effort has been made to obtain permission to reproduce the figures illustrated in this book. If any proper acknowledgement has not been made, copyright holders are invited to contact the publisher.

# Series editors' foreword

To an anglophone audience, the combination of the words 'French' and 'cinema' evokes a particular kind of film: elegant and wordy, sexy but serious – an image as dependent on national stereotypes as is that of the crudely commercial Hollywood blockbuster, which is not to say that either image is without foundation. Over the past two decades, this generalised sense of a significant relationship between French identity and film has been explored in scholarly books and articles, and has entered the curriculum at university level and, in Britain, at A level. The study of film as an art-form and (to a lesser extent) as industry, has become a popular and widespread element of French Studies, and French cinema has acquired an important place within Film Studies. Meanwhile, the growth in multi-screen and 'art-house' cinemas, together with the development of the video industry, has led to the greater availability of foreign-language films to an English-speaking audience. Responding to these developments, this series is designed for students and teachers seeking information and accessible but rigorous critical study of French cinema, and for the enthusiastic filmgoer who wants to know more.

The adoption of a director-based approach raises questions about *auteurism*. A series that categorises films not according to period or to genre (for example), but to the person who directed them, runs the risk of espousing a romantic view of film as the product of solitary inspiration. On this model, the critic's role might seem to be that of discovering continuities, revealing a necessarily coherent set of themes and motifs which correspond to the particular genius of the individual. This is not our aim: the *auteur* perspective on film, itself most clearly articulated in France in the early 1950s, will be interrogated in certain volumes of the series, and, throughout, the director will be treated as one highly significant element in a complex process of film production and reception which includes socio-economic and political determinants, the work of a large and highly skilled team of artists and technicians, the mechanisms of production and distribution, and the complex and multiply determined responses of spectators.

The work of some of the directors in the series is already known outside France, that of others is less so – the aim is both to provide informative and original English-language studies of established figures, and to extend the range of French directors known to anglophone students of cinema. We intend the series to contribute to the promotion of the informal and formal study of French films, and to the pleasure of those who watch them.

DIANA HOLMES
ROBERT INGRAM

# Acknowledgements

A debt of thanks is owed to the staff at the BiFi, Paris, and the BFI, London, for providing help, advice and the film stills to be used in this book. I would like to thank the British Academy for funding an essential research trip to Paris in 2002 and the School of Modern Languages, Queen Mary, University of London, for according me a semester of paid research leave in 2003, without which I could not have completed this project. My gratitude goes to all the staff at Manchester University Press for their kindness and professionalism.

For their advice, help and generous sharing of their film studies expertise, I should like to thank Lynne Higgins, Diana Holmes, Bill Marshall, Phil Powrie, Keith Reader and especially Sue Harris. For the invaluable loan of documents and films, sincere thanks are owed to Martine Beugnet, Catherine Cachart and Graeme Hayes; as well as to Jean Duffy, who shared her work on Leconte with me prior to its publication.

I must also record my special gratitude to Fiona Handyside, for alerting me to the dearth of theorization of the 'masculine masquerade', and for providing me with a hideaway in Devon to do some writing (in between rounds of golf); to Ben Dennis, for introducing me to the genre of the 'buddy movie', and for offering me his characteristically unique perspective on the condition of masculinity; and to Dany Nobus for devoting so much time to proofreading, transcribing, translating, providing psychoanalytic references, and generally aiding and abetting my efforts with unfailing patience, consideration and good humour. Finally, I am grateful to Patrice Leconte for the consistent kindness, generosity and enthusiastic support he has shown for this project.

This book is dedicated with love to M.B.D., 'L'homme sur le pont'.

# Introduction

Patrice Leconte appears to the world as a Janus-faced figure. On the one hand, he seems to wear the mask of the populist comfortably: he is widely known as the director of comic films such as *Les Bronzés* (1978); he is a regular maker of television commercials; and, in 1991, he launched a provocative attack on the French film critical establishment for its elitism and tendency to decry home-grown films, especially popular comedies. On the other hand, one might argue, his credentials could not be more highbrow. He served an apprenticeship at the prestigious IDHEC (Institut des hautes études cinémato-graphiques) and spent his early days working as a critic for *Cahiers du cinema*. He contributed to the collaborative film project *Contre l'oubli* (1991) in aid of Amnesty International, alongside such names as Jean-Luc Godard and Alain Resnais. He has written the screenplays for 16 of his own films and his work has been nominated for, and received, numerous awards, including several *Césars* and the BAFTA Best Foreign Language Film Award for the period drama *Ridicule* (1996). Elusive, pluralist, hard to pin down, part of the fascination offered by Leconte's persona and cinema alike is the fact that there is apparently more than one Leconte.

In the course of his 25 years as a filmmaker, Patrice Leconte has been perceived to undergo a metamorphosis from the 'popular' director responsible for the *bête et méchant*, off-colour humour of *Les Bronzés* to the art-house *cinéaste* who produced 'serious' and critically acclaimed films such as *Tandem* (1986), *Monsieur Hire* (1989), *Ridicule* and *La Fille sur le pont* (1999). However, this common perception of Leconte as a reformed character who made some puerile juvenilia before going on to enjoy a second career is largely unhelpful. Despite the obvious differences in cinematic techniques and production values between *Les Bronzés* and *Ridicule*, this neat division of his corpus into 'early' and 'late' Leconte is deceptive, and plurality rather than duality characterizes more accurately the maverick character of his filmmaking.

Leconte's body of films thus stands as an ambiguous and multi-valent corpus, which is both difficult to categorize generically and resistant to straightforward interpretation. Indeed, critics have been consistently divided regarding the quality and ideology of Leconte's work. His detractors have labelled him sexist, levelling accusations of sadistic misogyny at films such as *Le Mari de la coiffeuse* (1990) and *La Fille sur le pont*. Where films are critically acclaimed, reviews tend to focus principally on their formal aesthetic qualities (the rich script and visual humour of *Ridicule*; the stark aesthetic beauty of *La Veuve de Saint-Pierre* (2000)), without paying very much attention to their content or ethical standpoint. In the context of academic film studies in France, America and the United Kingdom alike, Leconte's work has received very little attention. Where mention is made of his name, it is often to illustrate a genre of cinema (the popular comedy via *Les Bronzés*; the *polar* via *Monsieur Hire*, the heritage movie via *Ridicule*) or an argument or principle of film theory, for example Guy Austin's discussion of *Le Mari de la coiffeuse* to exemplify the misogynist narrative convention of a film made from a male point of view, featuring a woman whose death provides narrative closure (Austin 1996: 54–7).

However, these references to Leconte's cinema for the purpose of neat taxonomy do not do him credit. In many cases, it is possible to submit that Leconte's films are not typical examples of a given genre or genres, but rather generic collages or, in some cases, filmic reflections on the means by which generic traditions are created. One can argue, for example, that *Tango* (1992), far from being just a road movie, uses techniques of parody, pastiche and intertextual citation (from the *bande dessinée* and from the cinemas of Bertrand Blier, Luis Buñuel and Alfred Hitchcock) to reflect upon both the construction of masculine archetypes and attitudes in twentieth-century culture, and upon conventions of filming. The blend of registers and styles, and the series of allusions and references to literary and filmic sources that structure Leconte's films, constitute an aesthetic that may be described as approximating the postmodern.

A careful assessment of Leconte's *œuvre* reveals a varied and generically disparate corpus of films, through which one can nevertheless trace significant lines of continuity and revision. These are found in his repetitive casting of certain actors (Michel Blanc, Jean Rochefort, Vanessa Paradis, Daniel Auteuil) and self-conscious exploitation of their star personae; in his development and reworking of key themes and ideas, across period and genre; and finally in his double refusal both to commit to a single genre and to obey generic conventions within any given film. Leconte's cinematic project is thus revealed as a highly paradoxical one: it is both refreshingly heterogeneous and yet surprisingly consistent and coherent.

To date, no study exists in English or in French which undertakes to submit Leconte's *œuvre* to rigorous critical reading, paying attention to its influences and intertexts in the cinemas of France and America, and tracing lines of disparity and continuity through the director's career. This, then, will be the aim of the present volume.[1] This book will provide close readings of a selection of films spanning the course of Leconte's *œuvre*, up to and including his latest film at the time of going to press, *L'Homme du train* (2002). Following an initial chapter which provides a descriptive and critical introduction to Leconte's career, four further chapters will be devoted to some of the principal themes, motifs and narrative devices which structure these films.

The second chapter will explore Leconte's use of comedy as a strategy for negotiating and navigating the subject's passage through the world. It will undertake a detailed analysis of the means by which Leconte uses visual gags, wit and verbal humour in his films. It will start by exploring Leconte's use of exaggerated physical stereotypes, bad taste and bawdy humour in *Les Bronzés*, an early film in the *café-théâtre* tradition. It will then go on to define repetitive strategies in Leconte's use of verbal wit from the popular comedies to the critically acclaimed and self-consciously intellectual comedy of eighteenth-century manners, *Ridicule*.

Chapter 3 will examine Leconte's representations of masculinity in relation to the rich and under-explored concept of the 'masculine masquerade', a term taken from psychoanalytic theory. I shall examine films, dating broadly from the middle period of Leconte's career to

[1] One full-length work on Leconte exists in French (Chantier and Lemeunier 2001). For an assessment of its strengths and omissions, see my review of this work (Downing 2003).

date, which are based on, or incorporate elements from, traditional masculine genres (the buddy movie, the road movie, the western). The chapter will examine the extent to which Leconte subverts the macho models offered by these genres, by allowing the spectator to witness gaps and fissures in the performances of masculine identities. It will also examine Leconte's use of male stars to reinforce, challenge or undermine notions of French masculinity. The audacious gesture of reuniting such a classical pairing as Belmondo and Delon in the 1998 film *Une chance sur deux* suggests a nostalgia for a lost epoch of French society and cinema as well as for clearly defined masculine roles.

The fourth chapter will examine the criticism often levelled at Leconte's cinema that it is excessively fetishistic and reveals a bias of misogyny. *Monsieur Hire*, *Le Mari de la coiffeuse* and *Le Parfum d'Yvonne* (1994) have all been read as operating according to the voyeuristic structure that privileges male scopophilic desire for the passive woman, as described by Laura Mulvey in her seminal article on narrative cinema (Mulvey 1975). The discussion will entail a brief rehearsal of the main tenets of feminist film criticism and of the predominant linking, within literary and cinematic narrative forms, of femininity and death. The question will be asked whether the three films under discussion may be read as *comments on* certain conventions of filmmaking, or whether they must indeed be understood as unquestioning endorsements of the tradition.

The final chapter will focus principally on Leconte's most recent films, *La Fille sur le pont*, *La Veuve de Saint-Pierre*, *Felix et Lola* (2001) and *Rue des plaisirs* (2001), which have in common a focus on unconventional relationships between men and women. I will argue that these films offer mature reworkings of the gendered dynamic explored in such films as *Le Mari de la coiffeuse*. The women portrayed in these films are complex, well-rounded characters whose motivations and personal histories are three-dimensional and yet elude total comprehension or assimilation. This means that neither the director, nor the viewer, nor the male protagonist may possess the female figures. The chapter will contain an exploration of the way in which these films are particularly self-aware with regard to the conventions of cinematic representations of women. It will examine the construction of several scenes that successfully manage to focus ironically rather than fetishistically on the female body.

A further element of complexity with regard to these most recent films lies in the ethical positions they take up around questions of responsibility, sacrifice and love. The work of French philosopher Emmanuel Levinas will be briefly explored here, as it offers a persuasive model with which to discuss Leconte's representations of relationships. Leconte, like Levinas, locates the ethical in the dimension of the personal encounter. In Leconte's late films, ethical questions are embodied in the figure of the couple that challenges heterosexual norms or risks self-sacrifice for the other. The chapter will close with a reading of *L'Homme du train*, which can be read both as a reworking of Leconte's earlier experiments in the male buddy movie genre, and as an extension of the exploration of ethical concerns visible in his late films about love between men and women.

The plurality, heterogeneity and blending of high and low cultural forms that characterize Leconte's corpus make it a filmic text which can most appropriately be explored via dialogue with a broad range of critical and theoretical positions. Thus, it is a deliberate strategy of the book to attempt to highlight the range of concerns in cinema theory and continental critical thought that exemplify, and can be said to parallel, the developments within Leconte's cinematic career. Thus, psychoanalysis, feminist theories of spectatorship, Foucauldian discourse analysis, deconstructive gender studies and Levinasian ethics suggest themselves at different moments as appropriate theoretical intertexts touching on the aesthetics, ethics, formal modes and themes raised in Leconte's cinema.

Following the model offered by philosopher Slavoj Žižek's recent writing on Jacques Lacan and Hollywood cinema (Žižek 1991 and 2001), I shall be arguing that Leconte's cinema, in both its 'popular' and 'artistic' modes, has significant resonance for wider debates in contemporary critical thought. Žižek's work seeks to subvert the generally accepted relationship of authority between high theory and popular cultural production, and to collapse the hierarchy of high and low cultural forms. For Žižek, 'Hollywood is conceived as a "phenomenology" of the Lacanian spirit, its appearing for the common consciousness' (Žižek 2001: xi). As well as undertaking close readings of Leconte's films as texts in their own right, and as texts existing and accruing signification in relation to other French and foreign films, this book will adopt an approach somewhat similar to Žižek's. Leconte's corpus, then, will be conceived as a 'phenomenology', for a

French (and sometimes foreign) common consciousness, of a range of concerns central to debates in modern critical theory, from the 1970s to the present date. The work of a 'popular' director – and more especially a director who problematizes a straightforward understanding of 'popular' and 'high' culture, as Leconte does – may be the most paradigmatic and appropriate corpus with which to explore the aesthetic and ethical debates of late modernity and postmodernity.

Leconte's status as an enigmatic director offering complex and paradoxical commentary on questions of social and sexual ethics is seldom given the serious consideration it deserves. The accusations levelled against him of misogyny, flippancy and an apolitical uncommitted stance – while not always unfounded – have served to blind the critically aware viewer to the broader potential interest of Leconte's cinema. I will argue that it is the criteria against which the films are being measured, rather than an innate lack of worth in the films themselves, that has provoked such a lukewarm and indecisive critical response to Leconte. However, it is not my intention to sweep under the carpet the politically problematic elements of this director's work. Rather, I propose firstly to offer a thoroughgoing and rigorous reassessment of the work of this multi-faceted and challenging director, and secondly to make a contribution to those practices of critical reading which contend that popular cultural production may offer a more accurate lens on to the workings of culture, subjectivity and the psyche than the most elaborate and complex social or psychological theories. It is my contention that Leconte's corpus, by dint of its famously unclassifiable, multiple and diffuse qualities, is one of the most fruitful and underexploited sets of texts with which to pursue this critical agenda in a contemporary French context.

## References

Austin, Guy (1996), *Contemporary French Cinema: An Introduction*, Manchester, Manchester University Press.

Chantier, Pascal and Lemeunier, Jean-Charles (2001), *Patrice, Leconte et les autres*, Paris, Séguier.

Downing, Lisa (2003), review of Pascal Chantier and Jean-Charles Lemeunier, *Patrice, Leconte et les autres*, *Modern and Contemporary France*, 11: 2, May, 217–18.

Mulvey, Laura (1975), 'Visual Pleasure and Narrative Cinema', *Screen*, 16: 3, autumn, 6–18.

Žižek, Slavoj (1991), *Looking Awry: An Introduction to Jacques Lacan Through Popular Culture*, Cambridge MA, Massachusetts Institute of Technology.

Žižek, Slavoj (2001), *Enjoy Your Symptom: Jacques Lacan In Hollywood and Out*, second edition revised with a new introduction, New York and London, Routledge.

# 1

# 'Leconte est bon!':
# the making of a director

## The early days

Patrice Leconte was born in Paris on 12 November 1947, but spent his entire childhood in Tours. Enamoured of the cinema from an early age, the boy from the provinces dreamed of acquiring a formal training in cinematography at the most prestigious school in Paris: 'J'étudiais les curriculum vitae des réalisateurs venus à Tours et je lisais: "Un tel a fait l'IDHEC". Pour moi c'était les dieux vivants qui avait fait l'IDHEC'[1] (Leconte 2000: 40). During the year of preparation for the concours (a competitive exam to allow entry to the film programme) he enjoyed rich pedagogical experiences, including visiting lectures by canonical names of French cinema such as Jean-Claude Carrière, and he relished the hands-on approach to the study of cinematography. Admission to the great school brought acute joy followed shortly by disillusionment and disappointment: 'L'IDHEC, le préstigieux IDHEC de mes rêves, se révèle un établissement poussiéreux et archaïque, sans contact avec le vrai cinema'[2] (Leconte 2000: 46).

Shortly after this bitter revelation, the student riots of May 1968 broke out. Leconte's professional training was interrupted by chaos and disarray in the name of a cause in which he did not politically or emotionally invest: 'comme je n'avais pas une conscience politique

1 'I studied the CVs of directors visiting Tours and I read: "so and so graduated from the IDHEC". For me, those who had been to the IDHEC were living gods'. All translations from the French are mine, unless otherwise specified.
2 'The IDHEC, the prestigious IDHEC of my dreams, was revealed as a dusty and archaic institution, nothing to do with the realities of cinema'

très aiguisée, et comme je continuais, suivant ma pente naturelle, à fuir tout conflit, les Événements de 68 m'ont plutôt fait peur, parce que le chaos ne m'a jamais convenu et que même le simple désordre me met mal à l'aise'[3] (Leconte 2000: 47). Perhaps these formative events go some way to accounting for the distaste and suspicion – discernible in Leconte's filmmaking, writings and interviews – in which he would henceforth hold elitist institutions, hierarchies and establishments, a dislike matched only by an apparently paradoxical mistrust of revolutionary agitation and all types of extreme political activism. Neither a conformist nor a rebel, Leconte seemed destined from an early age, then, to resist the labels and affiliations to which his peers were drawn and by which their work has come to be understood. Nevertheless, the diffident tone and self-confessed cowardice of Leconte's autobiographical statement cited above sit uncomfortably alongside the close involvement with an artistic environment of *contestation* and anti-bourgeois sentiment he would go on to pursue.

On leaving the IDHEC, Leconte worked as a film critic for *Cahiers du cinéma* and as a cartoonist for the fantasy magazine *Pilote*, before directing his first full-length feature *Les Vécés étaient fermés de l'intérieur* in 1975. The script of this farce about two bumbling detectives was adapted from the work of fellow *Pilote* illustrator, Marcel Gotlib, who co-signed the film. Heedless of his youth and inexperience, Leconte displayed considerable self-confidence in approaching Jean Rochefort, already a well-known face in French cinema, to star in his début feature. *Les Vécés* follows the suave Commissaire Pichard (Rochefort) and his subordinate Charbonnier (Coluche), as they investigate a bizarre murder case of a man (Roland Dubillard) who inexplicably exploded in a toilet stall that was locked from the inside. Despite widespread praise for the comic performances given by Rochefort and Coluche, the film was a box office failure and was generally hailed as a directorial flop. A reviewer wrote in *L'Express* of 'la réalisation fade de Patrice Leconte'[4] (*L'Express* 1976), while another concluded with the damning exhortation: 'Tirons la chaîne'[5] (*Minute* 1976).

3 'As I didn't have a particularly acute political consciousness, and as I continued, following my natural inclination, to flee any sort of conflict, the events of '68 made me rather afraid because I have always hated chaos and even simple disorder makes me somewhat uneasy'

4 'Leconte's bland direction'

5 'Let's pull the flush on it'. A less condemnatory assessment of the film might hold that it suffers from not having been sufficiently adapted from its *bande*

Following the commercial failure of *Les Vécés*, Leconte spent three years earning a living from cartoons and journalism, before making the fortunate acquaintance of the *café-théâtre* group *Le Splendid*. In 1978, he adapted their successful play *Amours, coquillages et crustacés* for the screen, under the title *Les Bronzés*. Leconte had the good fortune to have the strong recommendation of the troupe, who had admired *Les Vécés*, and who were able to convince their producer Yves Rousset-Rouard to invest in the young, virtually unknown director. The *Splendid* group, which counted among its members such names as Michel Blanc, Thierry Lhermitte, Josiane Balasko and Miou-Miou, also collaborated closely with film director Bertrand Blier, who worked to promote and encourage the troupe of young actors. All of them went on to enjoy successful careers in acting, direction and production. Moreover, Blier is credited with having renovated French cinema by bringing to the big screen specifically theatrical performance styles that originate in the burlesque tradition of the vaudeville-inspired *café-théâtre* (see Forbes 1992: 173 and Harris 1998: 96). While Blier's name is most often associated with this group of actors, it is frequently forgotten that Patrice Leconte was the first to direct them on screen in a film they themselves had scripted.

The influence on the young Leconte of both the *café-théâtre* milieu and Bertrand Blier's adaptation of its stylistic qualities for the cinema, cannot be underestimated, but nor is this influence a straightforward or unambivalent one. The *café-théâtre* tradition is 'a dramatic movement defined by satirical attack – a movement which mounted [...] a social and frequently forceful political critique of contemporary life' (Harris 1998: 89). Inspired by the revolutionary spirit of May '68, groups like the *Splendid* took as the target of their satire middle-class pursuits and ideals. Leconte's relationship with this *soixante-huitard* sensibility is, as we have seen, an ambiguous one. While vociferously denying any commitment to the political activism of the *soixante-huitards* that had interrupted his training at the IDHEC, Leconte was

*dessinée* origins for the demands and constraints of the screen. Gags that might amuse on the page fall somewhat flat in the context of Leconte's deliberately unobtrusive direction, helped only slightly by the counterpoint of an absurdly melodramatic musical score. When, in 1992 Leconte returned to the *bande dessinée* as a source of visual inspiration with *Tango*, his dynamic, pacy camerawork and editing, along with an audacious script, suggested much more effectively a cinematic approximation of an animated cartoon strip.

nevertheless clearly attracted to those counter-cultural forms – such as the *café-théâtre* and the satirical *bande dessinées Hara-Kiri* and *Charlie Hebdo* – that subjected bourgeois mores to merciless mockery.

*Les Bronzés* was a massive commercial hit, which brought the talents of both Leconte and *Le Splendid* to the attention of a mainstream viewing public. A total of 2,182,000 spectators saw *Les Bronzés* in France, which constituted a financial killing for the producers, director and actors.[6] The success of the film, and of its sequel the following year, *Les Bronzés font du ski* (with viewing figures of 1,354,900), proved a mixed blessing for Leconte, as it brought him a measure of commercial success and recognition, while simultaneously stamping him with the label of 'popular' comic filmmaker, which he would find hard to shake off. Indeed, for many, Leconte's name remains synonymous with *Les Bronzés* to the present day, at least in France.[7]

Over the next few years Leconte made three further comic films *Viens chez moi, j'habite chez une copine* (1980), *Ma Femme s'appelle reviens* (1981) and *Circulez, y'a rien à voir* (1983), all of which starred Michel Blanc, featured other *Splendid* actors, and were produced by Christian Fechner. Leconte has described this trio of films as 'film[s] de producteur'[8] (Leconte 2000: 119), owing to Fechner's detailed involvement with the projects and generous, comprehensive financial management.[9] While it is fairly standard for American producers to

6 A low budget film such as *Les Bronzés* would be considered a success if it attracted viewing figures in excess of a million. To hit the two million mark was therefore a triumph. As the production values of Leconte's films rose, however, so did the stakes. *Une chance sur deux* (1998) pulled in just over a million spectators, but still made a financial loss. *La Veuve de Saint-Pierre* (2000), the film with the highest production costs of Leconte's career to date, required over two million just to break even. (All viewing figures cited in this book are taken from Leconte 2000.)

7 The persistence in the popular cultural imagination of Leconte's happy – if hopeless – band of holidaymakers can be amply illustrated. When, in the summer of 2001, 'Paris Plage' (an artificially constructed beach resort on the right bank of the Seine) was opened, several publications advertising this conceptually exciting virtual holiday space, which promised Parisians the exoticism of sun and sand without the inconvenience of leaving the city, illustrated their features with images from *Les Bronzés*.

8 'producer's films'

9 Christian Fechner was responsible for the production of six of Leconte's films to date. As well as the three comedies with *Le Splendid*, he produced *Les Spécialistes*, *Une chance sur deux* and *La Fille sur le pont*.

be heavily involved in the direction their investments take, it is unusual in a European – and particularly in a French – context, where the tendency is to perceive the director as the author of his or her work and the producer as a mere financial agent without the right to artistic input.

These films made under the 'Fechner system' enjoyed a certain amount of popularity. *Viens chez moi* returned impressive viewing figures (indeed higher than *Les Bronzés*), with *Ma Femme s'appelle reviens* and *Circulez, y'a rien à voir* slightly lower, but each still exceeding a million spectators. They also mark important milestones in Leconte's development as a director. His foregrounding of Anémone's character in *Ma Femme s'appelle reviens* – the first female protagonist in his corpus to be at all fleshed-out – paves the way for later female incarnations, such as Adèle in *La Fille sur le pont* (1999), with whom she shares a boundless sexual appetite and suicidal tendencies. However, for the most part, these films enjoyed a lukewarm critical reception, particularly *Circulez, y'a rien à voir*, in which Jane Birkin was miscast as an untouchable *femme fatale*, a role which the glacial icon of French femininity, Catherine Deneuve, had turned down (see Leconte 2000: 133–6).

In 1984, a project came along that allowed Leconte to branch out by making a film in a radically different genre from the comedies for which he was known. Fechner approached him with a project that involved teaming Bernard Giraudeau, who had appeared in *Viens chez moi*, with Gérard Lanvin, in an action movie to be set on the Côte d'Azur. While the film's concept was fully formed in advance by Fechner ('assumant à 100% un travail de producteur à l'americaine'[10] (Leconte 2000: 140), a final screenplay was arrived at only after considerable pains. The text of *Les Spécialistes* (1984) was the result of a collaboration between the director and producer, two writers (José Giovanni and Bruno Tardon), Michel Blanc and Patrick Dewolf. The latter, as well as becoming a personal friend, would work closely with Leconte on the writing of several later screenplays. The result was a fairly formulaic buddy movie, which nonetheless bears analysis for its subtly subversive presentation of masculinity (see chapter 3 of the present book). This – at first glance unremarkable – film became an unexpected and overnight success that smashed Parisian box office records on its opening, and was seen by a total of 5,300,000 spectators

10 'taking on board 100% the American conception of a producer's job'

during its run in French cinemas. Leconte's name was at last on the public's and the critics' lips for reasons other than his direction of *Les Bronzés*.

## Après *Tandem*

For many film critics and cinemagoers, Leconte's corpus divides neatly between the comic films of his 'apprenticeship', such as those made in collaboration with the *Splendid* company, and his mature, 'serious' output, usually thought to begin with *Tandem* in 1986 (though no doubt indebted to the box office success of *Les Spécialistes*, which assured Leconte's viability as a commercial director). *Tandem* is an odd, atmospheric and blackly humorous film, which narrates the relationship between an ageing radio game show host (Rochefort) and his sound engineer (Gérard Jugnot). The film struck an immediate chord with a French public who espied similarities between Rochefort's character and real-life veteran radio icon, Lucien Jeunesse, host of *Jeu des milles francs*.

The mood in which critics received *Tandem* was, for the most part, one of delighted surprise: 'Patrice Leconte n'avait pas laissé jusqu'ici un sillon bien profond dans l'histoire de notre cinema. On est donc tout surpris de lui trouver ici une autre dimension'[11] (Macia 1987). Others were less disparaging of what went before, but agreed nonetheless on the quality of the 'new' Leconte: '*Tandem* est épatant'[12] (Chazal 1987). In a characteristically humorous tone, Leconte has rejected the notion that his career divides neatly into these 'non-serious' and 'serious' cycles: 'Je ne voudrais pas qu'on dise qu'il y a un avant *Tandem* et un après *Tandem* comme dans les pubs d'amaigrissement [...] Les choses sont beaucoup plus floues'[13] (Leconte 2000: 69). Indeed, the premise behind *Tandem* had fascinated Leconte as early as 1981, when he first worked on a prototype of the screenplay entitled *Chers amis, bonjour!*. One of the major difficulties Leconte

11 'Patrice Leconte hadn't left much of a mark on the history of French cinema up to now. It is therefore surprising to find a whole new dimension to him here'
12 '*Tandem* is astounding'
13 'I wouldn't want it said that there is a before *Tandem* and an after *Tandem*, as in those advertisements for weight loss products. Things are much more fluid than that'

faced was finding a producer willing to fund a film based on such an apparently thin and eccentric premise. While Fechner and several others turned him down, Philippe Carcassonne, who would go on to produce several of Leconte's most recent and most successful films, accepted the challenge.

The success of *Tandem* is due in no small part to Leconte's fruitful manipulation of the unlikely partnership of Rochefort and Jugnot. The motif of the mismatched pair, physically characterized by their disparity in height and build, visually chimes with earlier 'odd couples' Rochefort and Coluche in *Les Vécés*, and Blanc and Giraudeau in *Viens chez moi*, but achieves a hitherto unanticipated psychological depth. The relationship depicted is underscored by a bleak poignancy and pessimism as well as an obvious comic value.

This reworking of the relationship between certain actors and character types in the interests of increased psychological sophistication and narrative complexity was also the force behind Leconte's next film project *Monsieur Hire* (1989). Michel Blanc – formerly the clumsy, pallid holidaymaker of *Les Bronzés*, the lazy lascivious sponger of *Viens chez moi* and the sexual loser of *Ma Femme s'appelle reviens* – was reborn in Leconte's adaptation of Simenon's novel *Les Fiançailles de Monsieur Hire* (1933) as an enigmatic scapegoat, bearing associations of sinister sexuality and a quality of painful loneliness. Yet, crucially, the ghost of his former incarnations remains, merely recast in a different aesthetic and generic mode: the clown and loser of comic filmic manifestations transmutes into the tragic anti-hero as Leconte adopts the mantle of *noir*.

*Monsieur Hire* attracted much critical praise, confirming and reinforcing Leconte's newfound label of 'serious director'. Indeed, the film bore witness to several innovations of direction style. As well as casting Michel Blanc in his first 'straight' acting role and revealing his capacity to portray extraordinary qualities of emotional depth, it permitted Sandrine Bonnaire to incarnate a more complex female role than had previously been seen in any film by Leconte. The man's man – or perhaps more accurately the boy's boy – of French comedy thus began to treat the question of female subjectivity. He states: 'à partir de *Monsieur Hire*, j'ai éprouvé le besoin de travailler autant avec des actrices qu'avec des acteurs'[14] (Leconte 2000: 126).

14 'starting with *Monsieur Hire*, I felt the need to work with actresses as much as with actors'

Leconte continued in the vein of introspective, melancholic films about men and women with the idiosyncratic and semi-autobiographical *Le Mari de la coiffeuse* in 1990, and the dreamy and atmospheric *Le Parfum d'Yvonne* in 1993, a cycle only interrupted by his return to the exuberant comic mode and *bande dessinée* aesthetic of his earlier years with the release of *Tango* in 1992. However, despite its formal and generic differences from the films that immediately precede and follow it, *Tango* shared in common with *Monsieur Hire*, *Le Mari de la coiffeuse* and particularly *Le Parfum d'Yvonne*, the tendency to win Leconte a new accusatory label on the part of critics and reviewers: that of a woman-hater.

An article appearing in *Le Monde* described *Tango* damningly as 'une fable misogyne'[15] (Heymann 1993). Leconte has argued that *Tango*, far from advocating the machismo displayed by its characters, is in fact an ironic critique of those attitudes, meaning that the film contains 'un message quasi féministe'[16] (Leconte 2000: 240). This is an argument that has been generally poorly received. However, it is a persuasive one in the light of Leconte's rejection of hegemonic discourses and hierarchies, and his tendency to voice his dissent by means of ludic parody and exaggeration, techniques he borrows from the *café-théâtre*. Describing the misinterpretation of *Tango*, Leconte wrote: 'il m'est arrivé la même mésaventure qu'à Coluche qui fut taxé de racisme pour des sketches qui, pourtant, le dénonçait en en proposant la caricature'[17] (Leconte 2000: 226). The problem described by Leconte is the same problem faced by any artist who chooses to critique an ideology by means of parody or other imitative techniques: its success relies upon an audience receptive to the irony of the presentation and sensitive to the satirical ends to which certain discursive codes are being put. Unfortunately for Leconte, it seems that too often his films have been encountered by those with a tendency to read literally the content of a work, and to interpret description as endorsement.

The association of Leconte's name with misogyny was put on hold in 1995, when he turned back to the male friendship model with *Les Grands Ducs*, a tribute vehicle uniting three veterans of French

15 'a misogynist fable'
16 'an almost feminist message'
17 'I had the same trouble as Coluche who was accused of racism for sketches which, in fact, denounced racism by caricaturing it'

cinema: Jean-Pierre Marielle, Philippe Noiret and Rochefort. Despite the potential box office value of this line-up, the film was commercially unsuccessful and was critically derided on the rather nonsensical grounds that Leconte had foolishly cast actors too skilled to play convincingly the roles of failed actors (see Lennon 2003).

Leconte's fortunes changed in the most extreme way the following year, however, with the success of the costume drama, *Ridicule* (1996), featuring the impressive line up of Fanny Ardant, Charles Berling, Bernard Giraudeau, Judith Godrèche and Jean Rochefort. The film broke new ground for Leconte in several respects. It was the first film he was to direct without having written – or at least collaborated on – the screenplay (this was written entirely by Rémi Waterhouse, who approached Leconte about directing the project as he felt too nervous to take on the direction himself). It was also the first period film Leconte would direct and, if he is to be believed, the first screenplay with a historical setting that he did not find alienating and boring (Leconte 2000: 256). Thirdly, it was the first time that a film by Leconte would go on to win an award for which it had been nominated. In the national cinema industry awards – *les Césars* – *Ridicule* received nine nominations, which translated triumphantly into four awards, including the most prestigious award for best film. In previous years, *Tandem*, *Monsieur Hire* and *Le Mari de la coiffeuse* had narrowly missed receiving the *Césars* for which they had been nominated.

In addition to this mark of national recognition, *Ridicule* was nominated for the coveted Oscar for best foreign language film, taking Leconte on a trip to Los Angeles, dressed from head to foot in complementary Cerruti, where he would be photographed with his professed fan Mick Jagger (see Leconte 2000: 13–18). Ultimately, the Oscar went instead to the Czech director Jan Sverak for *Kolya*, but not before Leconte had been hailed as a worthy ambassador of France, in letters from the *Ministre de la Culture* and the director of the *Centre national de la cinématographie* (see Leconte 2000: 15). For once, Leconte was not on the margins of the establishment, but its representative.

It may have surprised some when, following closely on the heels of *Ridicule*, Leconte returned to the genre of the action movie which had proved so successful with *Les Spécialistes* 14 years earlier. *Une chance sur deux*, like *Les Grands Ducs*, offered Leconte the opportunity to unite on screen canonical heroes of French cinema – this time Alain Delon and Jean-Paul Belmondo – for the purposes of fondly parodying their star personae and the generic conventions of the films in which they had starred in their heyday. The ambitious Delon-Belmondo vehicle also featured Vanessa Paradis as the archetypal daughter in search of the secret of her paternity. Leconte and producer Christian Fechner envisaged creating a nostalgic cinematic spectacle that would appeal to the popularity of the great vintage actors of the French *polar*. However the film, as well as failing for the most part to capture the imagination of the critics, drew disappointingly low box office numbers on its release in Paris (20,000, in comparison with 62,867 for *Les Spécialistes*), and overall the production suffered a considerable financial loss on this relatively high-budget project.

All was not lost in this venture, however, as Leconte's working relationship with Vanessa Paradis had proved so fruitful and dynamic that he went on to cast her as the lead in his next film, *La Fille sur le pont*, based on an original script by Leconte and Serge Frydman. This black-and-white film, made in the *cinéma-vérité* style, casts Paradis as a sexually promiscuous and suicidal girl, alongside Daniel Auteuil, as the knife-thrower down on his luck, who hires her as his target. The black humour of this scenario – made darker by the associations of erotic pleasure both participants are shown to derive from the knife-throwing act – raised again in certain quarters the murmurs of misogyny that Leconte had attracted with *Tango* and *Le Parfum d'Yvonne* (see Vincendeau 2000). However, other critics appreciated the postmodern intertextuality of the film (its *nouvelle vague* style and allusions; its blend of realism and fairy tale; its echoes of Fellini's classic Italian neo-realist film *La Strada* (1954) and its same refusal on the director's part to interpret or explain character motivation and situation). However, despite the film's many qualities, the selection panel at Cannes were divided on its merit and, ultimately, it did not make it through to the final screening. During its release in France, it was attended by a respectable 600,000 cinemagoers and attracted relatively high viewing figures in the United Kingdom and America on its release abroad.

In an entirely fortuitous repetition of the casting move he had made strategically when he chose to direct Paradis in two consecutive films, Leconte found himself working again with Daniel Auteuil on

*La Veuve de Saint-Pierre* in 2000. This vehicle, which Leconte 'inherited' from Alain Corneau, marked Leconte's second incursion into the genre of the history film. It was also the first time he would work on a film with a *mise en scène* that is distant in both time and place (a nineteenth-century French-Canadian island). Additionally, the project offered him the opportunity to fulfil a longstanding desire to direct Juliette Binoche (Leconte 2000: 328). While the casting of the roles of the Captain and his wife Madame La had already been finalized by Corneau, the part of Neel Auguste, the third point in the love triangle around which the film pivots, remained to be filled. For this role, Leconte took the extraordinary step of approaching film director Emir Kusturica. Surprisingly, Kusturica accepted, and brought a remarkable quality of physical power and vulnerability to the role of the murderer undergoing rehabilitation. The film was a moderate critical success in France and abroad, with few commentators failing to appreciate the aesthetic qualities of the cinematography that managed to balance 'tight close-ups which [result] in a pervasive sense of suffocation' with 'panoramic views across the frozen landscape' (Witt 2000: 57). The story of the emotionally intense love triangle, however, did not unanimously convince. While for one critic 'Binoche et Auteuil rendent immédiatement palpable [...] la force [de l'] amour'[18] (Rouyer 2000: 28), another concluded that the film 'seldom delivers on the promise of emotional depth' (Witt 2000: 57).

In 2001, Leconte made two further films somewhat in the mould of *La Fille sur le pont* and *La Veuve de Saint-Pierre*, insofar as they can be described as unconventional, quirky romantic comedies, which play with the traditions of that genre. However, *Félix et Lola*, a pastiche of the *polar* set in a fairground, in which Philippe Torreton and Charlotte Gainsbourg play young lovers, and *Rue des plaisirs*, a sumptuous period piece treating a *ménage à trois* in a brothel, lack somewhat the verve and originality of *La Fille sur le pont* and the aesthetic perfection of *La Veuve de Saint-Pierre*. Perhaps deservedly, they failed to elicit either the commercial or the critical interest of the previous two films.

This may explain why, in 2002, Leconte turned away from fine portraits of desire between men and women in order to make a further film about male friendship. Animated by the audacious desire to

18 'Binoche and Auteuil convey palpably and with immediacy the power of love'

create a scenario that would unite popular French singer Johnny Halliday with Leconte's *acteur fétiche* Rochefort, the director approached Claude Klotz for ideas. The script that resulted was written with the two actors' personae and performance styles firmly in mind, a strategy that paid off when Halliday was awarded the Prix Jean Gabin for best actor. Like *Les Vécés* and *Tandem*, which had already cast Rochefort as one half of an 'odd couple' the film plays for effect on the disparity between two protagonists. However, the play of contrast in question does not simply rely on the juxtaposition of mismatched physical types for comic effect, as in earlier films. Instead, it draws on subtle differences in lifestyle, education, self-stylization and the metropolitan/province split. As well as portraying these individual differences, it focuses on the common experience of ageing and mortality, treating, sensitively and in some depth, an issue that Leconte had previously sketched in *Tandem* and exploited for primarily comic effect in *Les Grands Ducs*. In sum, *L'Homme du train* (2002) is an exceptionally mature film about maturation, in which Leconte reassesses some of the key concerns and themes that run through and draw together his corpus to date.

## Leconte and the landscape of contemporary French cinema

As even a brief survey of his career and filmography to date can illustrate, Leconte's films tend to fall outside of recognized categories and genres in French film, such as the post-'68 political film, the *noir* thriller and the heritage movie, even as they flirt with, acknowledge or gesture towards them. Leconte's identity as a director has a fragmented aspect, suggested by the number of different genres he has worked in and borrowed from, and the variety of direction styles that have influenced and continue to influence his work.

The contention that Leconte has made two types of film, one highbrow and critically respected, one lowbrow and popular but critically decried, has general currency. However, the neat mapping of these trends on to his early/late career does not bear close scrutiny. A critically deplored film such as *Les Grands Ducs* was made after *Tandem*, *Monsieur Hire* and *Le Mari de la coiffeuse*. A film generally acknowledged as undistinguished such as *Une chance sur deux* succeeded the highly acclaimed and prize-winning *Ridicule*. Moreover, those films that failed to appeal to the critics have not always, by contrast, appealed to the 'grand public'. *Le Parfum d'Yvonne* was both a relative box office failure and critically decried, at least in France.[19]

What is more, it is not so easy to separate out the influences that shape Leconte's filmmaking into 'immature' and 'mature' modes. A hybrid mixture of impeccable *auteur*ist apprenticeship and popular cultural credentials characterized from the outset Leconte's cinematography. While indebted to the *bande dessinée* and the vaudeville comic tradition, he also counted among his influences from his earliest days François Truffaut, Godard and Claude Chabrol ('je suis un enfant de la nouvelle vague ... ils étaient fous, géniaux et fabuleusement inspirés',[20] Leconte 2000: 44). Close on their heels come Eric Rohmer, Jacques Rivette and Jean-Daniel Pollet; Milos Forman and Roman Polanski; Woody Allen and Hitchcock (Leconte 2000: 52). If Leconte's cinematic vision blurs 'high' and 'low' art by adopting equally the stylistic and visual features of cartoon book and *cinéma-vérité* masterpiece, the ideology and class affiliations subtending his project are no less fragmented or contradictory.

One might ask why, and for whom, this eclecticism should be a problem. Leconte identifies a dominant strand in the intellectual heritage of French culture that leads those educated in that tradition to expect consistency and recognizable identity within a single artist's work: 'Il est dangereux, au pays du cartésianisme, de bouleverser les categories'[21] (Leconte 2000: 226). Indeed, this passion for taxonomy is often visible in the rhetoric of critics attempting to get to grips with Leconte's work, as the following example from *Cahiers du cinéma* demonstrates: 'il est difficile d'assigner le film [*Tandem*] à un genre, comique triste ou comique absurde, comique poétique, bien peu comique malgré tout'[22] (*Cahiers* 1987: 59).

If his penchant for plurality has annoyed the critics, it has, by contrast, equipped him to respond to opportunities for collaborative work. Leconte has contributed to two portmanteau films. The first, *Contre l'oubli* (1991), is a collection of shorts by thirty directors to mark

19 It would appear that this film enjoyed greater popularity and success in Argentina, Japan and the United Kingdom (Leconte 2000: 240).
20 'I am a child of the New Wave ... They were mad, brilliant, fabulously inspired'
21 'It's dangerous in the land of Cartesianism to overturn categories'
22 'it is difficult to assign a genre to the film: tragic-comic or absurd-comic, poetic-comic, not all that comic after all'

the thirtieth anniversary of Amnesty International. Leconte's contribution was a film of Guy Bedos addressing Mikhaïl Gorbachev in Moscow's Red Square. The second, *Lumière et compagnie* (1995), invited contemporary directors to take up the camera of the Lumière brothers, on the occasion of the centenary of the birth of cinema, and to make a film lasting the duration of a roll of film from the 1890s. Leconte chose to depict the passage of a train into the railway station at La Ciotat, in homage to the Lumières' seminal footage. These portmanteau films are not Leconte's only recent work outside of narrative cinema. As well as making numerous commercials for television, he has written a one-off episode *Toi, si je voulais* (1988) of the popular television series *Sueurs froides*, inspired by and dedicated to Alfred Hitchcock, and co-produced by long time collaborator Christian Fechner. He has also worked in investigative television journalism, exemplified by the 1998 documentary examining a rare and under-researched disease, *La Maladie orpheline*.

Despite the prolific disparity of his creative activities over the past decade, one can observe that in the last few years Leconte's narrative filmmaking seems to have settled somewhat into a pattern. His latest works are *films intimes* which share thematic and structural traits in common, even as they continue to differ formally, generically and aesthetically (compare and contrast, for example, the slick, black-and-white, New-Wave-tribute aesthetic of *La Fille sur le pont* with the sumptuous, rich colours of *Rue des plaisirs* or the stark, cold vision of *La Veuve de Saint-Pierre*). However, the concentration upon the minutiae of friendship, the betrayals and sacrifices of love affairs and the apparently trivial details of everyday encounters, draw together Leconte's most recent works and can appear to constitute a provocative rejection of the concerns animating the wider community of contemporary French filmmakers.

The 1990s in France saw the emergence of a trend of *cinéma engagé* of the social realist type, dealing with problems of urban violence, social dispossession and ethnic marginalization in France. Mathieu Kassovitz's *La Haine* (1995) and Erick Zonca's *La Vie revée des anges* (1998) are probably the best-known examples. It is tempting to interpret Leconte's own output during this period as a gesture against the grain, as witnessed by the fact that his later films are much more deliberately evacuated of socio-cultural reference points than even the early comedies such as *Viens chez moi*, which was widely recognized by critics as a comment – albeit a comic one – on the high unemployment and financial disenfranchisement of the urban young that was a feature of life in the 1980s.

However, if Leconte's most recent films eschew social realism, it is not because he favours instead the glossy aestheticism of the *cinéma du look*, exemplified by the films of Jean-Jacques Beineix (*Diva* 1981) and Luc Besson (*Nikita* 1990). Glamour and sheen are no more the staple ingredients of a Leconte film than gritty urban realism or the deprivations of youth culture. Instead, in his choice of *mise en scène*, Leconte tends to focus for inspiration on stylized worlds of performance and/or entertainment (the court in *Ridicule*, the circus in *La Fille sur le pont*, the fairground in *Félix et Lola*) or else on the banal realities of everyday provincial life and the predictable rituals and unexpected encounters it entails (days on the road and nights in shabby motels in *Tandem*; the rituals and routine of a small town in *L'Homme du train*). Paradoxically, these two modes are not incompatible with or in opposition to each other, since one of Leconte's greatest achievements, as I shall try to demonstrate in this book, is to reveal cinematographically the performativity of the everyday; the extent to which identities and lives are constituted as poses, performances, repetitions and deceptions at every moment.

Finally, if Leconte's films are preoccupied with sex, as has sometimes been claimed, he has nonetheless refused to capitulate to the recent trend for explicit erotic films, such as Catherine Breillat's *Romance* (1999), or films blending hardcore sexual action with violence, for example *Irréversible* (Gaspar Noé 2002). Leconte's appeal to eroticism in recent films like *Félix et Lola* or *Rue des plaisirs* is deliberately coy, muted and romantic. Indeed, one cannot help but note that his most recent films are among the least sexually explicit of his career. (Compare and contrast, for example, the *pudeur* of *Rue des plaisirs*, despite being a film set in a brothel, with the unashamedly fetishistic camerawork and nudity of *Le Parfum d'Yvonne* from eight years earlier.) Such are the subtle and perverse methods of resistance and rejection of dominant trends employed by the most mild-mannered and gentle provocateur in French cinema today.

## Leconte against the critics

In 1991, Leconte's name hit the headlines when a letter he wrote to the Société des Auteurs, Réalisateurs, Producteurs (ARP) went astray and landed instead on the desk of the newspaper *Libération*. Leconte's letter consisted of an invitation to his fellow filmmakers to meet in order to reflect upon what he perceived as the negative bias displayed by French film critics (in such different publications as *Télérama, Le Monde* and *Libération*) against the national industry. Leconte's letter, printed in *Libération*, read as follows:

> Depuis quelque temps, je suis effaré de l'attitude de la critique vis-à-vis du cinéma français. Je ne me sens pas plus visé qu'un autre (plutôt moins d'ailleurs) mais je lis simplement ce qui est écrit ici et là sur nos films. Certains papiers, qui ressemblent à autant d'assassinats prémédités, me font froid dans le dos, comme si leurs auteurs s'étaient donné le mot pour tuer le cinéma français commercial, populaire, grand public. Je ne sais pas ce que nous pouvons faire face à cette situation critique (le mot est amusant). J'ai bien quelques idées, mais je ne sais pas si elles sont bonnes. J'aimerais en parler avec vous de manière informelle. Merci de ne pas me laisser seul avec ma colère et ma perplexité.[23] (*Libération*, 25 November 1991)

The gauntlet thrown down by Leconte was taken up by 50 or so of his colleagues in ARP, which in turn led to equally impassioned responses from the critics under attack.

The debate that ensued was wide-ranging in its implications and was avidly followed by the French public, with each assertion and repost faithfully reported in *Libération* over the period October to December 1991. While some journalists praised Leconte for his bravery in voicing what was clearly a shared anxiety within the industry, certain film critics marshalled the language of anti-censorship, claiming that Leconte was attacking free speech or else they accused him of

---

23 For some time now I have been outraged by the attitude of critics towards French cinema. I don't feel myself to have been more attacked than anyone else (in fact rather less). I simply read what is being written in various places about our films. Certain documents, which resemble so many premeditated assassination attempts, chill my spine, as if their authors had decided to kill commercial, popular, populist cinema. I don't know what we can do in the face of this critical situation (excuse the pun). I do have a few ideas, but I don't know whether they are good. I would like to speak with you about this informally. Thank you for not leaving me alone with my anger and perplexity'

demanding an unethical privileged protectionism for the national industry, without regard for critical integrity.

Another accusation levelled at Leconte, and one which must have stung particularly acutely, was that his 'cri anti-critique'[24] was the tantrum of a spoilt child. As a filmmaker in one of the few countries to implement a governmental policy of offering subventions to the national film industry, Leconte was portrayed as an over-privileged and ungrateful bourgeois, and contrasted, for example, with film-makers in other countries, working with miniscule budgets and often in political regimes that repressed and censored freedom of expression, especially when they detected seeds of political dissent. The implication was obvious: the sort of popular narrative films made by Leconte, treating comic or personal – and therefore 'trivial' – subject matter certainly did not merit any special courtesy from critics. Indeed, by extension, the suggestion was that French directors should just be grateful to be monetarily assisted in producing their consumer goods without expecting to be critically acclaimed as well (see Goudet 1991 and Séguret 1991).

The demands of the ARP were formulated and drafted at their meeting on 4 November, and released to the world on 25 November with the publication in *Libération* of the filmmakers' manifesto 'Nous cinéastes'. They cited, as evidence to substantiate Leconte's initial claim, such 'titres chocs' as 'Pourquoi le cinéma français est nul',[25] taken from *Figaro Magazine*. They called for the establishment of a critical etiquette outlawing 'cette sémantique de la haine et du mépris'[26] and also demanded a ban on the common practice of publishing damning reviews of a new film up to two weeks before it appears in cinemas, thus potentially prejudicing its chance of a fair assessment by the viewing public and damaging box office takings.

To respond to the accusation that they were insular spoilt children demanding critical protectionism as well as state funding they wrote: 'Qui d'autre que les cinéastes français ont eu l'idée géniale de [...] montrer dans un festival prestigieux comme Cannes des films de cinéastes étrangers et qui a permis d'en découvrir des dizaines et des dizaines [...] comme Manoel de Oliveira, Mike Leigh, Pedro Almodóvar,

24 'cry against the critics'
25 'Why French cinema is crap'
26 'this rhetoric of hatred and contempt'

Jane Campion ...'[27] In describing this gesture of solidarity made by French directors to their foreign counterparts, the authors of the manifesto sought to stress their allegiance to their fellow artists and to refute their alleged occupation of the territory of complacent privilege and commercialism.

The 'affaire des critiques', as it has come to be known, put Leconte in the spotlight so prominently that widespread speculation regarding his position was inevitable. Was Leconte voicing an authentic and valid objection to a vicious prejudicial trait in the establishment, or merely expressing bitterness and frustration at the somewhat uneven (and, indeed, often hostile) reception that his own films had enjoyed? Certain of Leconte's accusations, however, are beyond dispute. His charge that the highbrow French cinema press, exemplified by *Cahiers du cinéma*, tends to treat popular home-grown comedies with a disregard bordering on contempt is both widely acknowledged and can be seen to reflect a general attitude within the industry. This phenomenon has even been dubbed the 'complexe Coluche', so named after the iconic 1970s comic actor, who received only one award in the whole of his career, for the uncharacteristic role of a cynical, hard-bitten policeman in Claude Berri's 'serious' film *Tchao Pantin* (1983) (see Harris 1998: 88). That the industry could ignore his major contribution to French comedy bears telling witness to the extent to which that genre is marginalized and accorded low cultural value.

Whatever the merits of the dispute, the director's resentment of the critics, and their awareness of his antipathy, did not quickly fade away. In 2000, Pierre Murat wrote acidly in *Télérama* (one of the publications named in Leconte's original letter): 'Depuis une polémi-que récente et grotesque, on sait Patrice Leconte extrêmement vulnérable aux reproches qui lui sont faits'[28] (Murat 2000). Murat then goes on to decry *La Veuve de Saint-Pierre* in the following – coruscating – terms: 'C'est donc avec le plus grand ménagement, une estime intacte, voire une pointe d'amitié jusqu'alors inexprimée,

---

27 'Who, if not French filmmakers, had the wonderful idea of showing at a prestigious festival like Cannes films by foreign directors which allowed for the discovery of scores of names such as Manoel de Oliveira, Mike Leigh, Pedro Almodovar, Jane Campion ...'

28 'ever since his recent grotesque polemical statement, we have known that Patrice Leconte is extremely vulnerable to the criticisms made of him'

qu'on prend le risque de lui annoncer l'atroce vérité: le lyricisme, c'est pas son truc'[29] (Murat 2000).

In the same year, Leconte's autobiography appeared, in which he wrote with equal vehemence:

> Je mesure aujourd'hui, étant donné le peu de considération que j'ai vis-à-vis des critiques, le paradoxe d'avoir débuté comme tel. [...] Les *Cahiers du cinéma* ont, depuis, systématiquement maltraité tous mes films. [...] il n'est pas réaliste de penser que tel grand cinéaste ne fera toute sa vie que des chefs-d'œuvres, et que tel autre ne fera que des merdes. Ce manque de discernement, lié à un total manque de générosité, me fait horreur.[30] (Leconte 2000: 53)

The irony underlined by Leconte of having been in his time both a critic and filmmaker, and his insistence on the unfairness of the impossible standards of consistent excellence demanded by critics, are right at the heart of Leconte's concerns and anxieties as a film-maker. Refusing to make the same kind of film twice in a row, refusing to obey rigid generic precepts, and refusing to stem the tide of a restless hunger to make film after film – as many as one or two per year in recent years – Leconte's maverick, chameleon approach can suggest an antidote to the sterile perfectionism and exacting *auteur*ist standards that many associate with the French film establishment and its feared band of critics.

### References

*Cahiers du cinéma* (1987), 'La Langue au chat', 397, June, 59.

Chazal, Robert (1987), '*Tandem*', *France-soir*, 17 June.

*L'Express* (1976), '*Les Vécés étaient fermés de l'intérieur*', 12 January.

Forbes, Jill (1992), *The Cinema in France after the New Wave*, Basingstoke and London, Macmillan.

29 'It is therefore with the greatest of tact, my esteem for him undiminished, indeed in a hitherto unexpressed gesture of kindness, that I take the risk of announcing to him the appalling truth: lyricism is just not his bag'

30 'I am aware today, given the little respect I have for critics, of the paradox of having started off as one myself. *Cahiers du cinéma* have, ever since, systematically mistreated all of my films. It is not realistic to think that such and such a great director will in his whole life only make masterpieces while another will only make shit films. This lack of discernment, in tandem with a total lack of generosity, horrifies me'

Goudet, Stéphane (1991), 'La Critique au bûcher', *Libération*, 3 November.

Harris, Sue (1998), '"Les Comiques font de la résistance": Dramatic Trends in Popular Film Comedy', *Australian Journal of French Studies*, 35: 1, 87–100.

Heymann, Danielle (1993), 'Une fable misogyne de Patrice Leconte', *Le Monde*, 6 February.

Leconte, Patrice (2000), *Je suis un imposteur*, Paris, Flammarion.

Lennon, Peter (2003), 'Don't Shoot the Director', *Weekend Guardian*, 29 May.

Macia, Jean-Luc (1987), '*Tandem* de Patrice Leconte: Et à demain si vous le voulez bien', *La Croix*, 18 June.

*Minute* (1976), '*Les Vécés étaient fermés de l'intérieur*', 14 January.

Murat, Pierre (2000), '*La Veuve de Saint-Pierre*', *Télérama*, 19 April.

Rouyer, Philippe (2000), '*La Veuve de Saint-Pierre*: La force du destin', *Positif*, May, 471, 28–9.

Séguret, Olivier (1991), 'Le Cri de l'anti-critique', *Libération*, 6–7 November.

Vincendeau, Ginette (2000), '*La Fille sur le pont*', *Sight and Sound*, June, 44.

Witt, Michael (2000), '*La Veuve de Saint-Pierre*', *Sight and Sound*, September, 56–7.

1 *Les Bronzés* (1978): feats of physical agility

2 *Ridicule* (1996): games of verbal dexterity

**3** Three men in a 'road movie' (temporarily going to seed): Lhermitte, Noiret and Bohringer in *Tango* (1992)

**4** Two men and a 'daughter': Delon, Paradis and Belmondo in *Une chance sur deux* (1998)

**5** Monsieur Hirovitch: the man behind the window (Michel Blanc in *Monsieur Hire*, 1989)

**6** Monsieur Leconte: the man behind the camera (during the filming of *Le Mari de la coiffeuse*, 1990)

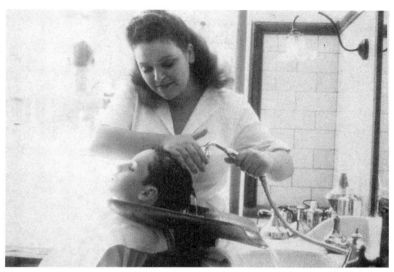

**7** Antoine's original love object: Madame Schaeffer (Anne-Marie Pisani) in *Le Mari de la coiffeuse* (1990)

**8** The object refound: Mathilde (Anna Galiena) shears an adult Antoine (Jean Rochefort) in *Le Mari de la coiffeuse* (1990)

**9** The female fetish object: the body of
Yvonne (Sandra Majani) in *Le Parfum
d' Yvonne* (1994)

la
sur

**10** Deconstructing fetishism: Adèle (Vanessa Paradis) the knife thrower's 'target' in *La
Fille sur le point* (1999)

34

11 The ethics of coupledom: Auteil and Binoche in *La Veuve de Saint-Pierre* (2000)

12 Encountering alterity: Madame La (Binoche) and the murderer (Emir Kusturica) in *La Veuve de Saint-Pierre* (2000)

## 2

# Comedic strategies:
# from *Les Bronzés* to *Ridicule*

J'ai parfaitement conscience d'être à chaque instant virtuellement
ridicule, mais je n'en ai plus peur. (Leconte, cited in Frois 1996)

(I am perfectly conscious of being ridiculous virtually all the time, but
I am no longer afraid of it.)

In an interview conducted to mark the screening of *Ridicule* at Cannes,
a journalist asked: 'comment passe-t-on des *Vécés étaient fermés de
l'intérieur* à *Tandem*, en passant par *Monsieur Hire*, *Tango* et aujourd'hui
*Ridicule*?'[1] (Frois 1996). Leconte appears to accept absolutely Frois's
observation that the films she names could not have less in common,
when he responds: 'Je vous l'accorde. J'ai un parcours totalement
incohérent!'[2] However, despite the journalist's consternation in the
face of Leconte's eclecticism, and the director's willing assumption of
that label, humour is a staple ingredient of all the films she names,
and will play a vital role in even the most dramatic or quasi-tragic of
Leconte's films such as *Le Mari de la coiffeuse* and *L'Homme du train*.

In response, then, to the common (mis)perception of Leconte as a
director who performed an about-face in order to become a serious
*auteur*, I will attempt to argue in this chapter that Leconte's specific
uses of comedy, throughout his filmmaking career to date, form a
recognizable continuum and can therefore – to some extent – be read
as an *auteur*ist signature. Although there is no doubt that the quality
of Leconte's films is inconsistent and that his humour has evolved

1 'How does one get from *Les Vécés étaient fermés de l'intérieur* to *Tandem*, via
*Monsieur Hire*, *Tango* and now *Ridicule*?'
2 'I'll grant you that. My trajectory is totally incoherent'

from the *bête et méchant* comedy of the 1970s *café-théâtre*-inspired films to a more sophisticated type of ironic and parodic humour in later works, the fundamental use to which Leconte puts humour is consistent and may best be defined as strategic. I will explore the strategic uses to which Leconte puts comedy, by means of a brief assessment of his early film *Les Bronzés*, which will then be put into dialogue with what is widely considered Leconte's most serious and 'intellectual' film to date, *Ridicule*. The disparity in 'brow elevation level' between the early film and the later work is a deliberate strategic choice on my part, as I wish to explore previously unsung parallels in films with very different values of both ideology and production.

## Sea, sex and sun ...

In the opening scenes of *Les Bronzés*, a coachload of French holiday-makers arrive in Abidjan to be welcomed by a party of dancing, singing 'natives', naked to the waist except for garlands of flowers. As the holidaymakers descend, so does chaos. Rain pours from the sky, soaking men and women in a range of 'holiday' attire (including one exaggeratedly skinny man in a bathing costume). Belongings are dropped and cases fall open revealing underwear. The local inhabitants start to steal luggage. Fights break out. The optimistic song, that promised 'sea, sex and sun' as the credits rolled minutes earlier, could not now seem more inappropriate.

This tableau exemplifies in various ways the humour that characterizes the early comedies of Leconte's career, made in collaboration with the *café-théâtre* group *Le Splendid*: it includes racial and physical stereotypes, exaggerated or grotesque dress and appearance, physical comedy, slapstick, the subversion of expectations, and a play on cliché. It also announces certain comic motifs that will be repeated several times in the film (unexpected showers that drench the *dramatis personae*; a visual play on physical clumsiness and the tendency to drop objects). A more detailed consideration of some of these comic features, and their function in the film, will offer insight into the key stylistic performance features of the *café-théâtre*, and will also identify strategic deployments of comedy that persist in Leconte's later films, even as they are revised and reworked according to the demands of genre.

Stereotype is one of the primary comic devices used in *Les Bronzés*. The racial stereotype of thieving black natives, the first with which we are presented, may at first appear to suggest a troubling attitude of racism on the part of the filmmaker. However, this assumption would rely on the understanding that what is presented on the screen can be read as representation in the realist mode, and bearing the stamp of authorial endorsement. Instead, *café-théâtre* comedy employs a type of humour known as 'derision', which is defined as 'the mockery of what people take most seriously through the exaggeration of its absurd or foolish aspects' (Forbes 1992: 175). Thus, the spectacles presented to us are to be read as humorous illustrations of, or oppositional responses to, the ideologies of everyday life that otherwise pass as naturalized. The 'natives' make several appearances throughout *Les Bronzés*, and each time they appear, they get the better of the French visitors or expose them to vulnerability or ridicule. In one scene of a native wedding, a bucket of water is tipped over the head of a white man while the natives stand laughing. In another scene, Jean-Claude (Blanc) attempts to take a Polaroid photo of a group of black children. However, his camera malfunctions and the bored children disperse. The attempts of the white French holidaymakers to 'consume' the culture of the 'exotic' location and to fix the image of the other are thereby consistently undermined. In this way, the rules according to which this game of stereotypes works are quickly made transparent: the object of mockery is not directly the individual or group being stereotyped, but rather the ideology that constructed the stereotype in the first place. Stereotypes in *Les Bronzés*, and in other works of *café-théâtre* and *café-cinéma*, are not in the service of the perpetuation of common cultural prejudices and assumptions, then, but rather carry a deliberate shock value in the service of denaturalizing dominant ideologies.

A second strategic use of stereotyping is characterized by the exaggeration of the physical appearance of actors, exploiting corporeal and facial features, dress and mannerisms. Leconte makes full use of the setting on a beach to expose the body shapes and physical gestures of his cast in the service of visual contrast. The curvaceous Gigi (Marie-Anne Chazel) first appears attired in shorts and a T-shirt, at the same moment as Christiane (Dominique Lavanant) arrives wrapped in a blanket, and with an expression revealing extreme displeasure. When Gigi elbows her out of the way, in order to shake hands with a group of men, the theme of female sexual rivalry is made explicit. The use of – sometimes violent – physical gestures to convey attitudes of aggression and competition is one way in which this comedy literalizes the usually tacit motivations and tensions underlying social interaction, and places them at the surface. However, if it is females who are at first presented as rivals and contrasting 'types' in the film, the focus quickly moves to the observation of masculine types and male heterosexual rivalry.

Writers on the French comic film have commented that this cinematic genre has 'nearly always relied on male incompetence as a source of humour' (Powrie 1997: 11). Male incompetence in *Les Bronzés* is incarnated in the figure of Blanc's character, Jean-Claude. Exploiting the comic associations of Blanc's physical type (he is short and skinny with a balding head and a black moustache), the film reveals Jean-Claude perpetually trying – and failing – to impress sexually the women he encounters. In one exemplary scene, he stands behind Gigi and Christiane who are sunning themselves on the beach, and attempts to gain their attention by repeating the uninspired chat-up line, 'C'est quoi ton prénom?'.[3] The conceit of Blanc's unprepossessing appearance and gauche sexual approach are exaggerated for comic effect and lent a physical dimension, as the women do not simply ignore his advances, rather they fail even to acknowledge his presence. The scene is constructed with Blanc positioned ineffectually behind their seated forms, appealing fruitlessly to their turned backs. Jean-Claude's discomfort is increased by the fact that the women are discussing their preferred masculine physical type, a verbal sketch which contrasts sharply with the physical spectacle he presents: 'grand, exagérément musclé et surtout les cheveux blonds'.[4] The cruel humour of the episode reaches its climax with a further element of humiliation. When Jean-Claude finally gives up and makes his way to the water's edge having cursed the two women, he encounters a couple of men of precisely the type the girls were discussing longingly. Towering head and shoulders above him, they easily overpower him, tear off his bathing shorts, and make their way over to the waiting girls.[5]

3 'what is your name?'
4 'tall, extremely muscular and definitely with blond hair'
5 Michel Blanc's star persona would become synonymous with this archetype of sexually rapacious but eternally thwarted masculinity between 1978 and 1983, when he would star in five Leconte comedies. The formula varied little, though

If the scene in which Jean-Claude's trunks are removed associates him with an obviously sexual form of humiliation, he is not the only male type who signifies in this way. Gérard Jugnot's short, stocky, plump physique contrasts with Blanc's slight wiriness, but is no more a figure of conventional sexual attractiveness. His character Bernard's marital problems with Nathalie (Balasko) are literalized in physical gestures in the scene in which he takes part in a bizarre game, as part of the resort's entertainment programme. In this game, two participants with sticks dangling from the end of a length of string suspended between their legs have to knock a ball back and forth, while the third tries to get his stick in a bottle (see figure 1). The fact that Bernard does not win at this game of physical dexterity is suggestive of the lack of sexual prowess of which we suspect him, despite his repeated boasts to his wife that he feels equipped to try non-monogamous marriage. In the failed seduction rituals engaged in by the men of *Les Bronzés*, it is physical appearance, strength, style and physical agility that are foregrounded as important traits for attracting women, and that let these disadvantaged types down time and again. The power wielded in the cultural imaginary by myths of potent masculinity is mercilessly mocked in the film's visual humour.

*Les Bronzés* constitutes a sketch of the social mores of its time, using the techniques of an oppositional theatrical mode that is clearly identifiable as part of the post-'68 fashion for derisive social satire. Characterization is one-dimensional in *Les Bronzés* and Leconte's other early comedies. Rather than attempting to represent psychologically complex and well-rounded protagonists, these comedies present satirical sketches of the preoccupations of the average Frenchman of the 1970s and 1980s, sharply caricatured as 'types'. Some specific contemporary detail is discernable in the films (the post-sexual revolution fashion for partner-swapping discussed by Bernard (Jugnot) and Nathalie (Balasko) in *Les Bronzés*; the 1980s crisis of unemployment referenced in *Viens chez moi*); however, the anxieties that are most visibly foregrounded and stridently mocked – those having to do with the meanings and expectations of masculinity

---

occasionally his incarnation of comic failure would incorporate additional elements to that of sexual loser, as in *Viens chez moi, j'habite chez une copine*, where he plays an out-of-work loafer, who benefits shamelessly from the generosity of his best friend (Giraudeau) and his girlfriend (Thérèse Liotard).

and the vulnerabilities of sexuality – are not limited to a particular social moment, but have archetypal or universal resonance. What is most particular about *Les Bronzés* is the way in which it harnesses the exaggerated comical and satirical features of a tradition of popular oppositional theatre in order to treat questions of masculine identity, sexual ambiguity and troubled interaction, which persist as obsessively recurrent themes in Leconte's cinema. Of equal note is the fact that while Leconte would abandon his collaboration with *Le Splendid* in 1984, significant elements of *café-théâtre* comedy would continue to feed into apparently 'serious' films, and to provide the subversive drive of Leconte's narratives.

## The ridiculous and the sublime: the ethics of wit

*Ridicule* is the story of a nobleman from the provinces, Grégoire Ponceludon de Malavoy (Berling), who goes to Versailles to seek financial backing from Louis XVI in order to drain the pestilent swamps on his estate and stop his peasants dying of fever. However, appeals to humanitarianism do not work at the Court, which prizes one currency alone: wit. He soon discovers that the ability to ridicule the other verbally, while avoiding ridicule oneself, is the only way to impress.

With *Ridicule*, Leconte finally created a film that would recoup acclaim from audiences, academics and the draconian French critics alike. Incorporating the production values and high cultural-intellectual content beloved of the French heritage film – that most valued of national cultural exports – the prize-winning period drama *Ridicule* appears to stand alone in Leconte's *œuvre*. This, at least, is the common perception. In fact, where *Ridicule* stands out most starkly from Leconte's other films is not in its themes or cinematography, so much as in its reception. As well as being the most highly rewarded of all his films to date in terms of industry awards and critical acclaim, it has also probably attracted the most sustained and serious Anglo-American academic attention, with writers investing great interest in the status of the film's historical setting and in its exposition of the function of language.

One of the most controversial features of *Ridicule* is Leconte's vehement denial of any interest in making a film about the eighteenth century: 'je n'ai pas une mentalité d'historien [...] Je vais donc faire comme si j'ignorais que ça se passe à une autre époque que la nôtre'[6] (Tobin 1996: 26). In a recent article, Mireille Rosello has argued that Leconte's renunciation of historical fidelity is justified by his attempt to make a film that comments instead on current concerns in twentieth-century French society. She maps similarities between the themes of *Ridicule* and certain debates in the French press of the time regarding medical ethics and the honesty of fundraisers.[7] For other commentators, Leconte's version of the court of Louis XVI, structured around a man of power and his verbally dextrous courtesans, offers deliberate echoes of the governmental realities of 'le mitterandisme' (Chantier and Lemeunier 2001: 470–1). In these readings, the eighteenth-century setting becomes no more than a pretext for a concern with the present, and the story of *Ridicule* an allegory for contemporary social problems.

However, this may not be an adequate account of Leconte's project. He is no more interested in filming contemporary 'issues' than eighteenth-century ones, and has categorically stated that he had no wish to 'transformer *Ridicule* en un film à clé'[8] (Tobin 1996: 31). Instead, a given setting in the past – such as the Court of Louis XVI – just as much as a given setting in the present – such as a holiday resort – might be chosen because it allows Leconte to explore certain situations and modes of interaction that, for him at least, seem to have universal import. At first glance, the historical and social setting of *Ridicule* and the type of refined verbal humour employed in the script may seem as far removed as one could imagine from the *café-théâtre* comedic style discussed in the previous section. However, a closer analysis of the comic devices and performance styles exploited in *Ridicule* suggests a deliberate cultural transfer of influences. Intertexts that are both popular and highbrow suggest themselves as ways as reading – and reading against the grain of – *Ridicule*.

6  'I don't have the mind of a historian. So I'm going to proceed as if I didn't know that the events took place in a different century'

7  The events provoking these debates were the scandal involving maladministration at the Association of Research on Cancer and the 'affaire du sang contaminé', both in 1995 (Rosello 1999: 81-2). In addition, Rosello cites the general atmosphere of unease in France regarding AIDS in the mid-1990s and the fact that *Ridicule* appeared at Cannes a few weeks before the 1996 'Sidaction'.

8  'turn *Ridicule* into an allegorical film'

*Ridicule* sketches an imaginary world in which verbal humour is the weapon and bargaining chip of choice, and in which the rules of wit and social interaction are heavily codified by an etiquette of *bienséance*. Witticisms made at the court may be as cruel as the teller desires, but they must not be cheap (*calembours* are thought of as 'lower' than *jeu de mots*) and – as Bellegarde (Rochefort) warns Ponceludon – one must never laugh at one's own witticism. Thus, any notion of wit as something spontaneous or joyful is stripped away and the exigency to be amusing becomes a burden to be borne.

The court depicted in *Ridicule* takes the form of a confined, claustrophobic stage with a small but exigent audience, where success depends entirely on skilled performance. Describing the conditions of fringe theatre groups in the 1960s and 1970s, Jill Forbes has written: 'in a situation where resources were limited, the success of the performance depended on the actors' physical and verbal ingenuity' (Forbes 1992: 174). In conceiving of *Ridicule*, Leconte takes the comedic techniques that were developed as a pragmatic response to – and integral part of – the *café-théâtre*'s conditions of existence (restricted performance space, few props, small cast of actors), and imports them into a diegetic *mise en scène* of eighteenth-century intrigue. Similarly, where in the *café-théâtre* 'catch-phrases, clichés, slogans and aphorisms' were the tools of the trade (Forbes 1992: 174), so the Court rewards the ability to use language cleverly with favours, both social and monetary.

The fear of being ridiculed that animates the players at the Court is not a fear to be taken lightly. Ridicule kills on many levels in the film: a poorly received play on words can spell social death, as in the scene of the 'wit's supper', when the diner making the least well-received witticism is asked to leave the table and eat with the servants. At other moments, the stakes are higher and it is shown to kill literally, as in the case of the Baron de Guéret (Albert Delpy) whose shoes are stolen and burnt, moments before he is summoned to see the king. Unable to be received in this inappropriate state, and humiliated before his peers, this social assassination is later crowned by an act of suicide, when he is found hanging by the neck from a tree in the forest.

The film thus enacts a transubstantiation: words and wit become not mere ephemeral things one might say but things one *does* and by extension, who one *is*. Wit, rather than physical strength, is aligned with youth and masculinity in the diegetic world in question. The

Marquis de Bellegarde expresses frequent frustration that his mind does not work as quickly as it used to, meaning that his enemy the Abbé de Vilecourt (Giraudeau) is able to outwit and upstage him in the arena of the Court. The casting of Rochefort as Bellegarde is significant, as Rochefort is recognizable within Leconte's corpus as a star text connoting vulnerable masculinity (see pp. 67–9 below). Where in other films (*Tandem* and *L'Homme de train*), Rochefort is vulnerable owing to physical fragility, in *Ridicule* it is the dulling of his acid wit that connotes encroaching age.

Verbal dexterity is collapsed on to sexual virility in the Court milieu, while the failure of wit, and the ridicule which results from it, suggest impotence or castration. This is thematized in one dining scene, in which a member of the *Académie française*, who fails to produce a suitably sharp witticism, is mocked by Vilecourt in the following terms: 'c'est normal [...] on confie le serrail à l'eunuque'.[9] The lack of wit is swiftly translated into a lack of 'balls', so that being in controlled possession of words is revealed to signify equivalently with phallic masculinity. Vilecourt, as one of the most cruelly witty – and therefore popular – of the male courtesans is equated with heterosexual success, crowned by the fact that he is also the lover of the beautiful and brilliant Comtesse de Blayac (Ardant), the most influential person at Court.

The alignment of language and sexual prowess works on many levels in the film. The art of seduction is shown to mirror the art of wit. In the scene in which Ponceludon attempts to seduce the Comtesse de Blayac, she demurs, saying that it would not be the first time a man had tried to get closer to the king by sleeping with her. Yet, it is not this duplicity to which she objects, merely the fact that Ponceludon was too clumsy in his seduction attempt for the deception to be convincing: 'sachez mieux dissimuler votre dissimulation afin que je puisse m'abandonner sans trop de déshonneur'.[10] Again, it is the seamlessness of the lover/wit's performance, rather than sincerity, that is shown to count. Where, in *Les Bronzés*, Gerard Jugnot's character submitted to the potential humiliations of the holiday camp game involving a stick – positioned like a penis – dangling between

9  'It's not surprising … every harem has its eunuch'
10  'you must learn how to hide your deception so that I can give in to you without too much dishonour'

his legs, the threat of ridicule for the courtesans lies in the failure of the dexterity of wit. Thus, it is a short and neat step from the game with bodies and sticks that crudely and grotesquely apes sex in *Les Bronzés*, to the impotence feared in *Ridicule*, whereby virility is a matter of verbal and mental sleights of hand (see figures 1 and 2).

If wit is codified as phallic in the onscreen world, women are nevertheless shown as able to wield power. We come to understand that it is not Vilecourt's success at Court that has allowed him to seduce the Comtesse de Blayac, but rather that his success is due precisely to the influence of the Comtesse, who works to advance his social position. This is revealed in the scene of the 'game of epigrams', in which the courtesans receive pairs of rhyming words, out of which they have to make a verse in a given metre. The Comtesse, who is Vilecourt's partner in the game, cheats: she has her own set of rhymes tucked into the folds of her fan, and Vilecourt is able to produce perfect alexandrines based on them. Thus, the Comtesse's power is revealed as one of deception. There is a tension in the film between the social restrictions placed on women in the eighteenth century and their manipulation of social codes that allows them to overcome these restrictions. What is exceptional about the world depicted in the film is that it is one in which masculine success is achieved by what would traditionally be codified as feminine means: manipulation, deception, verbal sleights of hand, etc. By replacing the familiar association of masculine power and direct action with a worldview in which indirect action wields the greatest influence, the film effectively forces a reflection upon the gendering of power.

The question of economic wealth inevitably enters the discussion of sexual politics too. The Comtesse's status as a rich widow affords her a liberty that an unmarried woman could never attain. This is highlighted by the case of Bellegarde's daughter Mathilde (Godrèche), who considers marrying a rich elderly man, de Montaliéri (Bernard Dhéran), in order to be able to continue funding her scientific experiments in water immersion. Mathilde sums up succinctly the possibilities open to a young woman without an inheritance when she evokes poverty, the nunnery or a wealthy husband as her options.

Mathilde is constructed in the film as an antidote to the mores of the Court. She is the proponent of the discourse of scientific reason, brought up by a father influenced by Enlightenment philosophy, who accorded her freedom and education.[11] When Mathilde uses language to persuade, it is under the sway of reason, rather than wit. In numerous conversations with Ponceludon, who disapproves of her unconventional, unfeminine behaviour, she espouses a pragmatic rationality, such as in the following piece of dialogue regarding the freedom of women:

> Ponceludon: 'La Nature prévoyante a mis les crabes sous l'eau et les jeunes filles chez leur parents'.
> Mathilde: 'La Nature aussi a envoyé la fièvre à vos paysans'.[12]

Mathilde's retort neatly inverts Ponceludon's discourse that what is natural is inevitably good. Her response espouses the scientific logic: 'just because certain things happen in nature doesn't mean we should leave them like that'. At other moments, however, Mathilde will have metaphorical recourse to Ponceludon's language of nature, in an attempt to convince him of the wrong-headedness of seeking out the favours of the Court, when she warns him that rotten trees never bear fruit.

Two worldviews are thus represented in the film: the decadent, artificial milieu of the Court and the world of Enlightenment progress, figured as the meeting of nature and science. The two worlds are grafted geographically on to Versailles and the Dombes, between which Ponceludon can move. They are also grafted sexually on to the bodies of the Comtesse de Blayac and Mathilde, rivals for his love. A decision to take one or the other lover thus equates with a choice of ideology – the archaism of aristocratic privilege and its cruel coda of wit, or the citizenship of the new world order that is on the verge of being born. This gendering of mobility and stasis (whereby the man can move freely between worlds, while the woman is confined) is fairly conventional in narrative cinema.

11 Bellegarde justifies the permissiveness of his daughter's upbringing by citing the fact that she was born in the same year as Rousseau's *Émile*. Mireille Rosello has pointed out that this reasoning is somewhat problematic, as Rousseau clearly argued that women were made for the pleasure of men and would not have advocated educating a girl in the same way as Émile: 'Surely the Rousseau referred to here is a vague idea, a stereotypical allusion to a certain canonical eighteenth century: to view Rousseau as one of the most revolutionary thinkers, we somehow need to invent his radicalness according to today's criteria' (Rosello 1999: 85).
12 'Sensible Nature put crabs under the water and young girls at home with their parents'; 'Nature also sent the fever to your peasants'

However, it would be a mistake to read the film's attitude towards its female characters as conservative or traditional. The complex characterization of the Comtesse de Blayac and of Mathilde, and the way in which Leconte demonstrates the constraints placed upon each of them by the roles allotted to women in their social context, suggests that the film is underpinned by a serious feminist agenda. As well as the scripting of strong female characters, the film plays with the conventions of visual appearance to draw attention to, or to subvert, assumptions about gender.

The Comtesse de Blayac, aligned in the film with deception, persuasion and a brilliance of wit, is introduced by a scene in which her naked body is covered from head to toe in powder, after the fashion of the period. While all the courtesans appear with highly powdered faces suggestive of masks, this full-body carapace functions as a visual reminder of the Comtesse's seductive manipulations and the fact that the effectiveness of her identity-performance is linked to her seductive body as well as her seductive speech. The artifice of the appearance of a body coated in white powder reminds the viewer of the foregrounding of performance and appearance in the film, to the apparent exclusion of all else.

Mathilde's physicality is portrayed in a slightly different way. The configuration of the Mathilde–Ponceludon–Comtesse de Blayac love triangle is recognizable as a narrative convention from the genre of the romance. In traditional romance narratives, an innocent younger woman is almost thwarted in her project of marrying the hero by an older, sexually experienced *femme fatale*. This generic tradition would demand that Mathilde should appear as archetypically feminine. However, while Godrèche's physiognomy suggests innocence and fragility, certainly in comparison with the extraordinary strength of Ardant's facial features, Mathilde is aligned, by a series of visual and verbal devices, with agency rather than passivity. At one point, she strips off her dress (very décolleté and in a simple peasant style), in order to put on a grotesque and neutering diving suit and helmet, as different from the prescribed feminine attire of the epoch as one could imagine. The diving suit appears several times throughout the film, worn by Ponceludon, Mathilde, the deaf-mute Paul, and – in one particularly bizarre instance – a couple of rabbits, which Mathilde has placed in it to test its watertight qualities. Thus it connotes a non-gendered identity and suggests, in keeping with the enlightenment signifiers that accrue to Mathilde, the idealist pursuit of science.

The striking visual effect created by literalizing the Comtesse's association with artifice, and by dressing the girlish Mathilde in the diving suit, echoes techniques drawn from the tradition of burlesque physical comedy that the *café-théâtre* adopted. It has been noted that the *café-théâtre* and Blier's *café-cinéma* tend to subvert the semantics of gender performance by two major means. The first is the exaggeration of features and appearance in order to 'challenge the "reflection of life" common to the cinema' (Harris 1998: 93) and to create denaturalized stereotypes. The powdering of the Comtesse de Blayac suggests an extension of this device, as it exaggerates the ritual of the female application of cosmetics that is largely naturalized in cinema. The second is the attribution of non-standard dress or personality traits to recognizable (stereo)types. This is what is done to the archetypal virgin of the romance genre when she dons a diving suit and acquaints herself with the laws of physics. What is more, when Mathilde undresses in the presence of Ponceludon, it is not to attract his gaze and that of the viewer to her as spectacle, as cinematic conventions demand, but to reattire herself for the purposes of carrying out a scientific experiment. Thus, our expectations, based on our understanding of the 'rules' of spectacle, are undermined.

If *Ridicule* goes some way to denaturalizing gender identity, this is achieved by deploying techniques of physical performance used by the popular *café-théâtre*. Yet it also parallels the concerns of a discourse operating in the 'high cultural' sphere, that of deconstructive gender theory. This body of theory, exemplified by the work of Judith Butler, highlights the performativity of identities, and the contingent cultural meanings of bodies, rather than the innateness of essences (see especially Butler 1993). It offers a framework with which to refute Ponceludon's assertion that the same law of nature puts girls in their parents' control as puts crabs under water. Mathilde, an eighteenth-century enlightenment scientist, obviously cannot have recourse to theories of social constructionism with which to show up the fiction of Ponceludon's belief in the natural law of gender. Instead, the film's manipulation of Mathilde's and the Comtesse's appearance effectively *demonstrates* the constructed quality of identity, by employing techniques borrowed from an earlier performative mode.

It is not only in relation to gender presentation that *Ridicule* can be said to dramatize the concern of contemporary thinkers with denaturalization. This applies also to the conception of power presented in *Ridicule*. The depiction of the Court suggests two models to account for the workings of power. Firstly, we are presented with the power of the king, a power to bestow favours on subjects, or withhold them, at will. Secondly, we have the power wielded by the courtesans, which can be described as a network of influence in constant flux, in which strategic alliances form, disperse and reform in a constant attempt to amuse, impress, inspire jealousy, abet and convince the king. (For clarity, the two models of power may be described as 'monarchic power' and 'the power of influence'.)

These two functions of power are described by Michel Foucault (1976), who argues that their deployment in the modern West has been misunderstood: we assume that power is still with the king, while in fact it is 'exercised from innumerable points, in the interplay of nonegalitarian and mobile relations' (Foucault [1976] 1978: 94). The historical period evoked in *Ridicule* bears witness to the eclipse of an instance of monarchical power, as the aristocratic order is overthrown in the revolution of 1789, to allow for a citizenship in which power functions 'without the king' (Foucault [1976] 1978: 91). The revolution takes place towards the end of the filmic narrative, and its events are not depicted on screen. Instead, it is signalled in the film's final moments by scenes of Bellegarde, exiled to England to escape the Terror. On to a tableau of Rochefort, looking across the channel to France where Ponceludon and Mathilde have remained, Leconte mounts an intertitle informing the viewer that the draining of Dombes was initiated in 1793 by Citizen Ponceludon, hydrographer and state engineer. The revolution, then, effectively enabled the humanitarian project that the Court of Versailles refused to assist.

The staging of the workings of power in *Ridicule* suggests an argument to explain how this film, set in a particular fictional past, functions to illuminate the past and the present. Rémi Waterhouse's script and Leconte's direction are historically located in an epoch of power without the king, namely the late twentieth century. However, according to Foucault, we have not come to assume this historical reality, and we continue to behave as if the king were still there. The exploration of a monarchical past in decline allows for a retroactive exploration of the workings of both models of power. Foucault suggests that the king's power is symbolic and that it is an effect, rather than the cause, of the ideology of hierarchy. *Ridicule* performs a very Foucauldian gesture, then, as it shows that the courtesans create the king as a figure of power by means of their repetition of performances of self-abasement in his service. In a fit of despair and abjection, following the theft of his shoes, the Baron de Guéret, who will go on to commit suicide by hanging, rails against the king: 'Louis de France, souviens-toi que c'est la noblesse qui t'a fait roi'.[13] Read philosophically, rather than literally, this statement encapsulates perfectly Foucault's idea that we are mistaken to assume that 'the sovereignty of the state' is 'given at the outset' (Foucault [1976] 1978: 92), rather than constructed by our belief in it.

As well as affording insight into the relationship between discourse and power, *Ridicule* encourages reflection on the function of language and the relationship between linguistic utterances, acts and identity. In one scene, l'Abbé de l'Épée (Jacques Mathou), who runs a hospice for deaf-mutes where he teaches them sign language, presents to the Court a group of his pupils. When he poses to the Court the question: why do we, who can speak, develop intelligence, while these people do not?, one nobleman proposes the response – 'car il est écrit "au commencement, était le verbe"'.[14] The liturgical interpretation of language is that it is sacred, because given by God as a gift to mark the uniqueness of humankind. Furthermore, when the Abbé announces his intention to marry two of the deaf-mutes before God, the nobles erupt, and claim that it would be sacrilegious for one without speech to receive a sacrament.

The belief system piously invoked by the courtesans holds that language is the medium by which the subject not only interacts with the other, but has a transcendental relation with God, and therefore assumes 'humanness'. This tendency to locate subjectivity in language has a more contemporary – and secular – equivalent in linguistically influenced poststructural theories. For psychoanalytic thinker Jacques Lacan, access to subjectivity is dependent upon the child's entry into language: 'le sujet ne peut malgré Descartes être pensé, si ce n'est comme structuré par le langage'.[15] (Lacan 1977: 13–14). The ability to use language gives the subject access to the social order, which Lacan designates as the symbolic, a dimension in which

13 'Louis of France, don't forget that it is the nobles who made you king'
14 'because it is written: "at the beginning was the word"'
15 'the subject cannot, whatever Descartes might have written, be thought, if it is not as structured by language'

all experience is mediated through the prism of language, and all wishes, desires and wants must henceforth be symbolized.

To turn back to the scene depicting the presentation of the deaf-mutes at Court, it is significant that when the deaf-mutes show they can use sign language to be humorous as well to communicate – one boy makes a sign and the group dissolves into spontaneous laughter – the tone of the courtesans' objections turns from sanctimonious religiosity mixed with mockery to panic. When they demand to know the joke, the Abbé says that it doesn't translate, explaining: 'c'est un geste d'esprit'.[16] Bellegarde, Mathilde and Ponceludon are the only spectators to stand and applaud, while the others depart in high dudgeon. In this sequence, the emphasis on spoken language is subordinated to the efficacy of physical gestures. For the Court, the notion of wit without words is literally unthinkable.

The displacement of focus from the verbal to the physical sphere thus prefigures the climactic moment of the film, in which a physical rather than linguistic 'slip' makes Ponceludon the butt of ridicule. The film reaches its climax at the 'Wit's ball', an event which Ponce-ludon attends with his fiancée Mathilde. In a gesture of revenge, the scorned Comtesse de Blayac plots to have Ponceludon tripped during a dance. Ponceludon's fall, filmed in slow motion, and accompanied by a shrill inarticulate shriek, is presented as a physical manifestation of the verbal slips, or falls into silence, that have provoked ridicule throughout the film. Ponceludon's trip and scream represent a fall *outside of* discourse, an instance of what Lacan would term the 'Real', that is, an experience which is not symbolized.

A film which apparently forsakes physical comedy in favour of sublime wit, and foregrounds words over action, is ultimately revealed as intimately concerned with the body. The bodily is that realm which the controlled etiquette of the court attempts to refine, restrain, silence: in short to decorporealize, in the exquisite stylization of performance. However, the repressed body returns in *Ridicule* as the society's symptom, the underside of wit. The film is framed by moments of bodily excess: it opens with a scene in which the Chevalier de Milletail (Carlo Brandt) pays a visit to M. de Blayac (Lucien Pascal), in order to urinate on his frail, aphasic body. Significantly, aphasia is a condition in which the subject is robbed of speech,

16 'it is a play on signs'

making impossible any 'meaningful' repost. We learn that the scatological act of revenge is wrought because de Blayac once mocked Milletail when he fell during a dance. Rosello has already pointed out that this opening scene can be retroactively understood at the film's *dénouement* as a warning: Ponceludon's final social downfall will echo Milletail's earlier fall (Rosello 1999: 89–90).

The status of excessive corporeal gestures and scatological bodily functions in *Ridicule* is thus one of disruption and disharmony. The strict codes of Court life demand a rigid control over the body, which must be made into an instrument of performance; a perfect visual complement to verbal wit. This is seen in the elaborate powdering of faces and restraining of hair under wigs, in the gestures designed to accompany rhetorical flourishes, and in the imperative to laugh without showing one's teeth. However, these stylized modes of bodily restraint constantly fall apart, seen in the repeated motif of falling during dancing, in Guéret's emotional breakdown outside the king's chamber, and in the scene of urination.

The concentration on – often grotesque, excessive or obscene – corporeal acts and displays is also a feature of the *café-théâtre* performance style. In this context, they signify as 'mercilessly aggressive' gestures of 'iconoclastic irreverence' (Harris 1998: 89). The effect of these gestures and acts in the diegetic world of *Ridicule* is similarly to disrupt or subvert the social order. Even if, with the exception of the urination attack, the victim of the act tends to be the one who 'falls' out of the system, the system is nonetheless shaken by these deviations from the norm. The deaf-mutes cause so much suspicion among the courtesans primarily because they seem to offer a way of being that appears spontaneous and unfettered by strict rules of interaction. The laughter of the deaf-mutes is the only 'real' laughter to be observed in *Ridicule*, even if attention to comic technique is both the subject matter of the film and its means of execution.

Following the climactic moment of Ponceludon's fall, he attempts to address the company plainly, appealing directly to their conscience and humanity, and denouncing wit. However, he can only do this in the same medium (language) that the courtesans manipulate as their tool of power. The extent to which he is trapped in language is emphasized visually in the framing of the scene, which sees him surrounded by masked courtesans, claustrophobically hemmed in. Indeed, his speech, while trying to be transparent and direct, inevitably uses rhetorical devices. He says, 'Vous enviez l'esprit de Monsieur Voltaire. Le grand homme aurait pleuré lui, car il avait une ridicule sensibilité au malheur humain'.[17] This play on the word 'ridicule' is not a *jeu de mot* this time – a pun designed to impress and make the listener laugh – but an unintentional 'slip'. Ultimately, then, any attempt to communicate in language inevitably involves the mediation of sentiments in words, as well as unconsciously assumed rhetorical devices and styles, which – as Lacan would hold – construct the subject rather than being constructed by him. Thus, Ponceludon's decision to return to the countryside, and try to achieve his humanitarian project via the manual and intellectual labour of engineering, bears witness to the observation that the only viable resistance to discourse may well be action.

## Some concluding remarks

*Ridicule* is an extraordinarily hybrid film. It blends performance techniques lifted from the *café-théâtre* with a presentation of issues such as the function of language, power and ethics, that suggests an intertext with the thought of modern critical thinkers, Butler, Foucault and Lacan. Moreover, *Ridicule* constitutes a brave choice for a director of comedies. In this film, the social functions of humour, wit and laughter are stripped cynically bare. As the *café-théâtre* tradition uses exaggeration and stereotype to denaturalize assumptions about contemporary social types, so *Ridicule* puts the very function of humour and communication under the lens of deconstruction and examines them as performances. Leconte's choice of a setting distant in time makes sense most convincingly, perhaps, if we understand it as a device with which to allow this dissection of wit and interaction to take place under the most extreme and acute conditions.

For Leconte, 'le comique est fondé sur les situations et l'observation du quotidien'[18] (Leconte 2000: 130). Whether the everyday life in question is that of the present day, or of two centuries ago, seems to matter less to Leconte than the opportunity to explore the functioning of humour in social interaction. We have seen that the protagonists of

17 'you admire Voltaire's wit, but you would make Voltaire cry because he was ridiculously sensitive to human suffering'

18 'comedy is founded on the observation of situations in everyday life'

Leconte's films use humour primarily as a defensive, persuasive or ethical strategy for negotiating the demands of the social sphere and navigating their passage through the world. In Leconte's filmic universe, humour or wit become ways of attempting to deflect embarrassment or violence. I have also shown that Leconte uses humour to articulate some of the dilemmas of male heterosexuality and the social demands of masculinity, a thematic that paves the way for the discussion of Leconte's treatment of the male friendship movie to be undertaken in the next chapter.

## References

Butler, Judith (1993), *Bodies that Matter: On the Discursive Limits of Sex*, New York and London, Routledge.

Chantier, Pascal and Lemeunier, Jean-Charles (2001), *Patrice, Leconte et les autres*, Paris, Séguier.

Forbes, Jill (1992), *The Cinema in France after the New Wave*, Basingstoke and London, Macmillan.

Foucault, Michel (1976), *Histoire de la sexualité 1: La volonté de savoir*, Paris, Gallimard.

Foucault Michel ([1976] 1978), *The History of Sexuality 1: The Will to Knowledge*, translated by Robert Hurley, Harmondsworth, Penguin.

Frois, Emmanuelle (1996), 'Patrice Leconte: "J'aurais fait un bon courtesan"', *Figaro*, 9 May.

Harris, Sue (1998), '"Les Comiques font de la résistance": Dramatic Trends in Popular Film Comedy', *Australian Journal of French Studies*, 35: 1, 87–100.

Lacan, Jacques (1977), 'C'est à la lecture de Freud ...', in Robert Georgin and Jacques Lacan, special number of *Cahiers Cistre* (no. 3), Geneva, L'age d'homme, 9–17.

Leconte, Patrice (2000), *Je suis un imposteur*, Paris, Séguier.

Powrie, Phil (1997), *French Cinema in the 1980s: Nostalgia and the Crisis of Masculinity*, Oxford, Oxford University Press.

Rosello, Mireille (1999), 'Dissident Voices Before the Revolution: *Ridicule* (Leconte, 1996)', in Phil Powrie (ed.), *French Cinema in the 1990s: Continuity and Difference*, Oxford, Oxford University Press, 81–91.

Tobin, Yann (1996), 'Entretien avec Patrice Leconte: *Ridicule*, c'est le titre de ma vie entière', *Positif*, May, 25–31.

# Modes of masculinity

> Les hommes et les femmes ne sont pas faits pour vivre ensemble. (L'Élégant (Noiret) in *Tango*)
>
> (Men and women were not meant to live together.)

## The masculine masquerade

A large number of Leconte's films, particularly those made in the middle part of his career to date (the 1980s and 1990s), focus thematically and generically upon male relationships and foreground certain male actors (Jean Rochefort, Alain Delon, Jean-Paul Belmondo) in such a way as to contribute to, exploit or skew their existing star images. In his choice of generic mode, cast and subject matter, Leconte puts masculinity relentlessly on display.

It is my contention that Leconte's films demonstrate ways in which cinematic masculinity functions as a masquerade. The concept of masquerade, in the context of film criticism, developed in relation to theories of femininity. It originates in the psychoanalytic writings of Joan Rivière, for whom a masquerade of femininity is an excessive display of appearance and behaviour that are codified as feminine, performed by the female who fears retribution for a moment of assertive subjectivity (a moment of masculine appropriation) (Rivière 1929). She recedes from the illicit position of the speaking subject behind the acceptable mask of 'her' gender. Reading the masquerade of femininity in cinematic terms, Mary Ann Doane notes that it appears, paradoxically, both naturalized and yet strange or excessive.

It makes visible the gap 'between the woman and the image of femininity' (Doane 1988: 48–9).

Very little has been written, however, on the possibility of a male version of the masquerade.[1] Those who argue the masculine position does not require a masquerade because the man already occupies the role of the subject in the symbolic order forget that, in Lacanian theory at least, the possession of the phallus (rather than just the penis) is a delusional phantasy of masculinity rather than an attribute of it (Lacan [1958] 1966).[2]

Moreover, recent gender theory, particularly that of Judith Butler, contends that all gender meanings are conveyed and construed by codes of performativity. By extension, for Butler, all gender performance is drag, whether consciously chosen or unconsciously repeated, and any performance of gender is precarious, provisional and potentially traumatic: 'This "being a man" and this "being a woman" are internally unstable affairs. They are always beset by ambivalence precisely because there is a cost in every identification, the loss of some other set of identifications' (Butler 1993a: 126–7). Butler's understanding of gender identity as constructed by a series of repetitive performances for which there is no original in nature suggests a way of reconciling the notion of the masquerade – an excess of gender signification designed to account for a lapse or lack – with certain modes of cinematic presentation of the male.

There are two principal means by which Leconte denaturalizes filmic signifiers of masculinity in order to present masculine performativity or 'males in masculine drag' as an excess of signification and as a source of anxiety. The first involves a fragmentation and exaggeration of certain generic conventions that codify men in ways acceptable to, and commensurate with the aims of, the heterosexual order. The second relies upon a self-conscious manipulation of actors' performance styles and star images.

---

1 The most significant exception is Chris Holmlund's essay 'Masculinity as Multiple Masquerade' (1993). The article theorises that films in which Sylvester Stallone appears alongside a 'clone' (e.g. *Lock Up*, John Flynn and *Tango and Cash* Andrei Konchalevsky, both 1989) demonstrate a queer hysterical aesthetic of multiple masquerade.

2 Lacan proposes the term 'parade virile' as the male counterpart to the female masquerade (Lacan [1958] 1966: 695).

## Gender/genre trouble

Masculine genres originating in Hollywood (the western, the thriller, the road movie, the buddy movie) traditionally focus either on the figure of the lone hero or, in the case of the buddy model, on a pair of men who traverse danger and adventure together, and whose principal bond of loyalty is to each other. Variations on the buddy movie theme tend to portray a tough, experienced older man and a younger, headstrong apprentice figure. *Butch Cassidy and the Sundance Kid* (Hill 1969) and *Thunderbolt and Lightfoot* (Cimino 1974) are paradigmatic classics of the genre. This is a formula that Leconte borrows in *Les Spécialistes* and *Tandem*, but in such a way as to exaggerate or undermine the ideological underpinnings of this cinematic form.

Critics have commented upon the implicit homoeroticism of the buddy movie (Tasker 1993, Fuchs 1993, Wyatt 2001). In *Les Spécialistes*, Leconte plays on this silenced subtext with the result that what is usually repressed becomes explicit. From the opening scenes, the iconography of *Les Spécialistes* works to suggest a deep emotional link between the protagonists, Paul (Bernard Giraudeau) and Stéphane (Gérard Lanvin). They are prisoners, handcuffed together in the course of being transferred from one prison to another. When Paul, an accused cop killer who is really an undercover cop, overpowers one of the guards and makes his escape, Stéphane is literally bound to follow. The motif of being handcuffed together and on the run echoes, most famously, Hitchcock's *39 Steps* (1935) in which Madeleine Carroll finds herself cuffed to a suspected murderer. The mixture of tacit eroticism and menace that characterises the interaction of this Hitchcockian couple is only carried so far by Leconte, however. At first Paul is aggressive and dominant, threatening to 'casser les couilles'[3] of his unwilling accomplice unless he co-operates. Progressively, however, Stéphane asserts himself, telling him, 'j'aime pas tes méthodes'[4] and an equality is gradually suggested between them. By the time the physical cuffs come off (when they are rescued and sheltered by Laura (Christiane Jean)), they are nonetheless symbolically still yoked together. They sleep in the same bed and their body language (although Paul's is still more confrontational and aggressive) mirrors each other.

3 'break the balls'
4 'I don't like the way you do things'

The relationship that develops in the film between Paul, Stéphane and Laura offers a novel spin on the convention of the male friendship film. Traditionally, women appear in such films in roles which require them to do very little more than provide a nominal object of sexual desire for the male characters. The presence of such a woman, with whom one or both of the buddies sleeps, provides a guarantee of the heroes' 'heterosexuality' so that the real focus of the film's interest – the relationship between the men – can be freed from any suspicious taint of homosexuality. This mechanism is thus a pandering gesture to identificatory audience homophobia. This is the very mechanism that Eve Kosofsky Sedgwick brings to light in *Between Men* (1985), a study of representations of male friendship and rivalry in the modern period. Sedgwick argues that the woman in a love triangle is desired by the first man primarily *because* she is the object-choice of the other man. By having sexual contact with this object, the first man has access to the desire of the other man and sleeps with him by proxy, as it were. This is necessary, claims Sedgwick, in a society in which there is a radical – and artificial – discursive disruption in the continuum between 'homosociality' (sanctioned male bonding in the interests of societal progress) and 'homosexuality', which is despised (Sedgwick 1985: 1–2).

The 'threesome' in *Les Spécialistes* functions as a nod to – and a radical departure from – this model. Laura becomes an accomplice rather than a desired object: she agrees to shelter them in exchange for a share of the loot they will gain from their heist (though she does not get it in the end). Neither man sleeps with Laura as the filmic convention demands; rather she exchanges chaste hugs and kisses with them both in a relationship which is much closer to a sibling bond than an erotic attachment. What is more, although Laura is a conventionally beautiful woman, she is rarely the focus of the camera's attention. Close-ups of the two men's faces and bodies are much more frequent and attention is paid to their sartorial habits, as in the scene in which Stéphane chooses Paul's tie. Thus, Leconte effectively thwarts the expectations of the genre: he provides the required woman to deflect the homoeroticism of the male couple, but refuses to follow through with the however nominal (and misogynist) conceit of using the woman disingenuously as a sexual scapegoat.

The action plot of *Les Spécialistes* is routine to the point of being cardboard. Visually, the *mise en scène* and camerawork make it an exemplary and unexceptional heist movie/western, incorporating car chases, vistas of rough, wide-open terrain (the Côte d'Azur) and a familiar iconic language of good and bad, law-abiding and law-breaking (with the minor twist that one of the 'criminals' is really a cop). I would suggest that the banality of the action plot results from the fact that this element is what interests the director – and the spectator – least in the scenario being presented. The formal expectations of the genre are rigidly adhered to only in order to highlight more forcefully the level on which its ideology disintegrates.

This disintegration occurs most forcefully as the film approaches its close. Having secured the bag of money in the casino heist, the pair stand facing each other, deciding how to proceed. The camera lingers on point-of-view close-up shots of each man's face and eyes, as Stéphane asks Paul if he will come away with him. When he fails to answer (torn between desire and duty), Stéphane picks up the loot and walks away. Immediately Paul trains his gun on him, aiming it at his torso until Stéphane has disappeared through the door. As soon as he is gone, Paul's face breaks into fond laughter and then his head drops into his hands.

This scene demonstrates admirably the notion of the masculine masquerade I am proposing. The genre the characters are inhabiting demands that a confrontation between lawman and criminal take place over and above the personal emotions of the participants. Paul's empty gesture with the gun suggests his awareness of the symbolic import of their respective roles and the show of machismo occurs primarily to mask the – 'feminine' – surge of vulnerability at watching the other walk away. While a gun is probably sometimes just a gun, Paul's extremely symbolic and over-determined recourse to his in this scene suggests irresistibly a momentary attempt to shore up phallic power, to be seen as one *who has the phallus*: this pretence is the very logic of the masculine masquerade. However, his obvious lack of intention to use the gun/phallus and his breakdown into laughter signal forcefully the abandonment of the performative mask of macho confrontation; while the dissolution into gestures of despair shortly after highlights the emotional difficulty of the dissimulation.

The very final sequence of the film resolves these tensions in a triumphant subversion of the values of the genre. Paul and Stéphane are shown together again in a tight two-shot, riding side by side on the back of an open-air freight train. They wrap the chains designed for holding cargo in place around their wrists jokingly, in a parody of the cuffs that held them together in the opening scenes. But also, of course, the gesture suggests irresistibly a symbolic marriage. In confirmation of this impression, they then throw the bag of cash off the moving train, thereby discarding the generically sanctioned pretext for male partnership – the spoils of crime. As they lie down together on the moving train, the credits role.

Of all Leconte's buddy movies, this is the most extreme, but not the only case in which the homoeroticism of the convention is brought to the surface. *Tandem* also features more subtle examples of this strategy in its portrayal of the relationship between Jean Roche-fort as a radio presenter, Mortez, and Gérard Jugnot as his companion and sound engineer, Rivetot. In numerous scenes their relationship is portrayed as ambiguously codified either for another onscreen character or for the spectator. This is seen firstly when the couple needs to share a hotel room. The motivation is financial rather than sexual, but the insistence on a hidden reason that must not be spoken about (Rivetot is embarrassed by the state of the accounts) inevitably suggests the sexual realm. Secondly, a verbal joke on the part of Rivetot brings to the surface level of the text the erotic subtext that is always unspoken in the buddy movie. A girl asks Rivetot if he has any children, to which he comments: 'j'aimerais bien, mais Mortez veut pas'.[5] On one level, this merely suggests that working for Mortez takes up so much time that Rivetot has not been able to start a family. On another level it speaks the silenced fact that their relationship is the most important and affective in Rivetot's life (we know that he is more or less estranged from his wife) and it effectively inscribes the pair of men in the role of a married couple. Finally, and most significantly, the way in which Leconte films the two men is often connotative of deep intimacy. In the final frame, the two men sit talking in Mortez's new car. The camera focuses in close up on one man's profile then cuts to the other, so that they appear to be looking into each other's eyes: a piece of filmic grammar known as the shot/reverse-shot with an eyeline match, that is most often used when filming lovers.

Leconte is not the first director to make visible the silent homo-eroticism of the genre. Bertrand Blier's *Les Valseuses* (1973) includes the male rape of one 'buddy' by the other, a rape that is then recu-

5 'I'd like to, but Mortez is against it'

perated as just another part of male bonding: 'c'est normal entre copains'.[6] Blier thereby attempts to overcome what Sedgwick has termed the break in the continuum between homosociality and homosexuality by making gay sex a logical – literal – extension of the generic format. Filming a decade after Blier's exuberant satires, Leconte's buddy movies do not delineate the erotic subtext of male friendship quite so explicitly. Indeed, according to Guy Austin, 'Leconte does not challenge the form, he merely inhabits it' (Austin 1996: 56). However, I think Austin is much too hard on Leconte here. If Leconte's experimentations in traditionally masculine genres are less flamboyant than Blier's, Leconte nonetheless explores the sub-textual and silenced meanings of masculine interaction and desire in films by focusing on the excessive signification of heterosexual masculinity in such a way as to show up its gaps, as I have highlighted above. Moreover, far from rendering the silent erotics of the buddy movie as a dynamic of violation and macho violence, as Blier does when he films a rape between men, Leconte suggests a possibility of tenderness and emotional as well as erotic connection between men *despite* the macho settings. One could argue that, in this, *Les Spécialistes* is more subversive and less potentially homophobic than *Les Valseuses*.

*Les Spécialistes* and *Tandem* are ambiguous texts that are conventional enough to offer a mirror of the classic buddy movie format – a recognizable mirror of the heterosexual world – but subversive enough to show that what is reflected in the mirror is a mask, a performance of heterosexual masculine signification, grotesque and excessive enough to constitute an overcompensation for the lapse into a prohibited desiring position. If Blier's *dramatis personae* dissolve the binary divisions of the symbolic order, Leconte's – in *Tandem* at least – are still recognizably neurotic. I would not wish to argue that Leconte is by any means pursuing an agenda of gay activism here. However, I hope to have demonstrated that his vision is not nearly so heteronormative as has sometimes been assumed. Moreover, by filming challenging configurations of masculinity in a popular rather than high art cinematic genre (*Les Spécialistes* was, we must not forget, a record-breaking box office success[7]), Leconte undermines the notion

6 'it's ok between mates'

7 62,867 people saw the film in Paris, making it the best-attended feature since *L'As des As* with Belmondo in 1982 (*France Soir* 1985).

that ideological subversion is only possible in the context of *avant garde* filmic modes.

Where *Les Spécialistes* works to subvert the meaning of the buddy couple, *Tandem* deforms the convention of the male hero in a number of different ways. Specifically, the monolithic heroism of the classic buddy movie's elder male partner is undermined by continuous revelations of human weakness. Rochefort's ageing radio game show host, Michel Mortez is physically fragile (he faints several times), emotionally unstable (he is prone to panic attacks and histrionic outbursts) and sexually vulnerable (he confesses that 'les femmes m'intimident'[8]). Similarly his assistant, Rivetot (Jugnot) is not the lithe, attractive younger male archetype (Jeff Bridges's Lightfoot), but a short, stocky figure who is bizarrely prone to hallucinations of a red dog. Thus, the sheen of physical perfection and macho courage that accrue to the Hollywood buddies is supplanted in Leconte's version with a tragi-comic blend of pathos, eccentricity and appeal to the everyday.

The film works to highlight the schism between the vulnerable contingencies of phenomenological reality (illness, fear, sexual anxiety) and the opacity of surface appearance. This is achieved most obviously by having Rochefort play a performer, someone whose image is everything, and more specifically a performer aware of his fading popularity and the fact that his radio show is about to be taken off the air. Various performance techniques and narrative devices show up the *décalage* between Mortez's subjective reality and the appearance he shows to the world. When addressing members of the public (his fans, hotel employees), he delivers lines dramatically, with the charm of a public celebrity. He enunciates and inflects his words with panache, suggesting the acme of confidence. When in conversation with Rivetot, however, Mortez fluctuates between an unassuming modesty and outbursts of wild, uncontrolled anger or emotion.

Similarly, the extent to which the character's self-presentation is a chosen construct designed to shore up a lack of confidence and present a suave, sexually knowing façade is revealed by numerous means. Firstly, he confesses to having changed his name from Morteau to Mortez, as the Latin-sounding ending suggested a desirable South American-style virility. Secondly, in the interests of impressing an attractive woman he meets at a dinner party, Mortez pretends that

8 'I'm scared of women'

he is a guest in a luxury hotel rather than admit to the modest one at which he is really staying. Associations of an ideal masculinity – South American machismo and financial opulence – are thus donned like clothing to mask the symbolic dispossession of the fading star.

Leconte emphasizes these motifs of disguise and performance with certain visual techniques. Several times in the film Rochefort is shown observing himself in a mirror or other reflective device. In one scene he appears dispirited and lost. He looks in the mirror and begins to practise his fake celebrity smile which, when it falls from his face, reveals once again an expression of despondency. Here, Leconte highlights a very visible example of the masquerade of masculinity and this scene stands as a literal exposition of the silent mechanism it is treating. Indeed, film critics have picked up on the function of the mask in this film, one reviewer in *Positif* commenting, 'le film revêt l'aspect d'un documentaire sur le vieillissement de Rochefort, la décomposition d'un masque de Don Juan infantile (*sic*)'[9] (Sineux 1987: 64). Mortez is a figure who is about to slip outside of the accepted role filled by the male – that of the active subject with a successful career. Whenever he feels tempted to succumb to the fate that awaits him and to slip into passivity, the mask indicating self-possession and agency has to be pulled on again, in a gesture of pathetic over-compensation. The conceit of the performer whose career is at an end is one that Leconte reprises elsewhere, suggesting that it is a figure of masculinity with enduring appeal for the director. In his 1996 comedy, *Les Grands Ducs*, an altogether less complex film than *Tandem*, Marielle, Noiret and, once again, Rochefort – an impressive line-up – are cast as ageing and failed comedians, eager to perform together one final time.

In films such as these, the ideology subtending the genre of the buddy movie is subtly parodied such that action and physical prowess are replaced by the ability to perform, amuse, seduce or convince. Leconte thus replaces those attributes of masculinity, deceptively presented as natural and inevitable in the classic model (strength, courage, confidence), with repetitions, imitations, dissimulations and performances: qualities traditionally associated with the feminine masquerade. What this suggests, perhaps, is an awareness of the fragility of all performances of gender and identity. Although *Tandem* is a film about men, it shows inevitable human weakness being

9  'The film takes on the appearance of a documentary on the ageing of Jean Rochefort, the decomposition of a mask of childish Don Juanism'

compensated for, not by the codes of machismo but by the performative sleights of hand and adoption of suitably imperturbable masks that the subject is routinely called upon to perfect.

It is perhaps more counter intuitive – but not, I will argue, impossible – to isolate such a 'humanist' agenda in the road movie *Tango*, a controversial film that provoked much condemnation. *Tango* foregrounds the misogyny that is often the silent logic of the male friendship model, in which women are incidental to the plot and are instrumentalized as sex objects or victims. It achieves this foregrounding via a pattern of verbal humour and ironic reference to other cinemas, bringing to the surface a formerly repressed agenda. It is my contention that *Tango* has been much misunderstood by those who accuse it of perpetuating the misogynist discourse it is actually exposing.

Each of the principal characters of *Tango* performs an extreme and hyperbolic rhetoric of misogyny. Vincent (Richard Bohringer) is a pathologically jealous pilot who murders his adulterous wife. L'Élégant (Noiret) is a retired judge who lives alone with his cat and harbours particularly indulgent attitudes towards wife murderers. His son Paul (Lhermitte) is a serial adulterer who wants to have his estranged wife Marie (Miou-Miou) killed by Vincent. Wife murder, then, is the somewhat grubby grail sought by the three men who embark on this quest.

Misogyny and violence towards women are displaced in this film from the silenced, repressed shared object underlying the coda of male friendship to the most transparent level of discourse. 'Vous dansez bien pour un misogyne',[10] comments Madeleine (Godrèche), the young woman who goes on the road with our homicidal trio after shooting her husband. To this the judge retorts: 'J'aime les femmes mais je ne veux pas vivre avec'.[11] The constant references to the way in which men and women cannot live happily together satirizes the convention of the road movie which inevitably involves a retreat from sedentary life and associations of domesticity into an all-male, dynamic space.[12]

10 'You dance well for a misogynist'
11 'I do like women but I don't want to live with them'
12 This conceit is undermined when the three characters find themselves at a certain point without transport, in a field, and up to their necks in grass (see figure 3); their abandonment of 'civilized' life in favour of the idyllic green world is revealed as another kind of discursive myth or trap.

Godrèche's character functions interestingly in the film and is significant for any discussion of its alleged misogyny. She is accepted by the men as one of their number, by dint of the fact that she too has killed her partner (because he was unable to give her a child). The suggestion is that she has more in common with them than with the women they despise. In fact, the three male characters are hopeless idealists, driven in their relationships not by a serious attempt at intersubjectivity, but by impossible ideals which their partners inevitably fail to attain. Their acceptance of Madeleine into their company suggests that the real enemy of the trio is not women, but the social codification of romantic love and the imperative that relationships between the sexes should end in monogamy and marriage. In this, the film is anti-establishmentarian in a way that is reminiscent of Blier's social satires which replace the heterosexual couple with threesomes and other imaginative erotic configurations (e.g. *Les Valseuses, Tenue de soirée* (1986)). That *Tango* is a conscious homage to Blier's cinema is suggested both by the casting of Miou-Miou, one of Blier's major actresses, and by a scene in which Madeleine suggests that one of the men she is travelling with might like to give her a baby. This is a direct allusion to Jacqueline's request to lose her virginity to Jean-Claude and Pierrot in *Les Valseuses*. Leconte's reference to Blier here suggests a sympathy for the other director's project of problematizing heterosexual interaction.

Other noteworthy cinematic allusions in the film are to Hitchcock's *œuvre*. The early scene of Vincent's plane flying low over fields is reminiscent of *North by Northwest* (1959) (and suggests a link between Vincent and one of the least macho of all Hitchockian heroes, the mother-dominated character played by Cary Grant); while Vincent's later confession that he suffers from vertigo reminds the viewer of another Hitchcockian hero. *Vertigo* (1958) is in fact one of the most suggestive of *Tango*'s intertexts, even if only briefly referenced. Scotty in *Vertigo* is erotically obsessed with a woman in a fashion that resembles Paul's obsession with his wife Marie. In *Vertigo*, Judy (Kim Novak) impersonates Madeleine, the wife of a former colleague of Scotty, and then fakes her suicide to cover the murder of Madeleine. Once 'Madeleine' is apparently dead, Scotty becomes increasingly obsessed by her and devotes himself to trying to make Judy resemble the other 'dead' woman as much as possible. In the closing scenes of *Tango*, Vincent pretends to shoot Marie as Paul has instructed him to do. It is only once Paul believes Marie is dead that he realizes he still loves her. The parallel with *Vertigo* is striking: a faked death leads the male protagonist to fall further in love with the dead object, suggesting a tradition of representations of a pessimistic masculine logic of love that relies on the impossibility of consummation. But in *Tango*, all is performative and parodic. Whereas in *Vertigo* a suicide was faked to allow the real murder to be committed, in *Tango* the murder at the end is not real but a simulacrum. Thus, while echoing Hitchcock's thematic preoccupation, Leconte translates it to the level of a ludic repetition, a parodic acting out of that director's obsessions. Misogyny itself becomes an elaborate masquerade for the characters in *Tango*: a swaggering pose that masks the threat of emotional vulnerability and the ego-abyss of desire.

One further cinematic intertext offers illumination of Leconte's agenda. In a scene set in a luxury hotel, Paul is attracted by a stunning woman played by Carole Bouquet. Bouquet is, of course, best known for playing Buñuel's obscure object of desire, the role that subsequently inspired Blier to cast her as the too-beautiful woman in *Trop belle pour toi* (1989). In *Tango*, in acknowledgement of the fact that Bouquet connotes the eternal feminine, a personification of beauty without subjectivity, the character is not given a name. In the scene in question, Paul makes a wager with his travelling companions that he will be able to seduce the beauty. He admits to her the terms of the wager and she agrees to let him accompany her to her hotel room, in order to convince his friends that he has succeeded in his conquest. Once there, however, she reveals herself willing to go through with the sexual encounter for real. The *enjeu* of bluff and masquerade (in the lay sense of the term) does not end there. A humble, downtrodden looking hotel bellhop, played, significantly, by Jean Rochefort, is ultimately revealed as the husband of the mysterious beauty in the penthouse suite. He works in the hotel in order to support her extravagances and to be near her. The episode is undermining of the type of discourse to which it initially appears to appeal. The notion that the very ordinary Paul could successfully seduce the feminine ideal, the embodiment of beauty, at first appears to be a piece of male wish fulfilment of the crudest kind. However, the appearance of Rochefort and his revelation provides a back story to Bouquet's incarnation and relativizes the fantasy through parody. The price of marriage for Rochefort's bellhop is servitude to an ideal. The episode effectively mocks the very myth it at first appears to be reifying: the idealization of female beauty that puts the woman up on a pedestal (or up in the penthouse suite) reducing her subjectivity to objectification and her lover's subjectivity to the level of idolatrous slave. The sequence thus shows up the failure of intersubjectivity consequent upon the conventions of courtly love and marriage.

The reference to two filmmakers (Blier and Hitchcock) whose names have been consistently associated with misogyny, but who have recently been reread by critics as allusive and parodic,[13] reinforces the notion that *Tango* is a film about the mechanisms of misogyny and, more specifically, a film about the difficulty of locating the source of misogynistic discourse. It may not be where it is most often looked for (in certain male-authored works) but rather in the very discourses that appear to offer women security and affirmation (romance, marriage, domesticity, the family) and that provoke unreal expectations and mutual antipathy.

Thus, although *Tango* is certainly deliberately provocative and employs a shade of black humour that is not to everyone's taste, the discourse that operates at the surface level of the film is not in accordance with the overall narrative logic, which offers significant moments of subversion, disruption and dislocation. *Tango* shows how men and women are constructed as discrete categories of being and set in opposition with each other in a 'war of the sexes', not by natural design, but by the conventions of gender stereotyping which force individuals into binary roles. Moreover, it suggests that women are culturally conditioned as weaklings and victims by the discursive constraints involved in the social institution of marriage. By offering the alternative (however morally dubious) categories of those who attempt to escape these discourses of entrapment by murderous means (including Madeleine), Leconte surprisingly breaks with the fixed opposition between man/woman as inevitable enemies, which

13 Recent scholarly work has suggested that the apparently misogynistic representations in these filmmakers' work should not be read as straightforward symptoms of the directors' own agendas or worldview; and indeed that to accept the films as bearing a misogynistic message is to read them incorrectly. For a feminist revisionist reading of Hitchcock see Modleski ([1988] 1989). For a study of Hitchcock as a director whose work bears queer viewing practices, see Samuels (1998). For a re-evaluation of Bertrand Blier's alleged misogyny, see Harris (2001).

naturalized misogynist discourses presupposes. His glance at the – however flawed – possibilities of interaction outside the conventions of the heteronormative economy suggests a utopian desire to focus on a communality of human experience rather than a woman-hating separatist agenda.

## Manipulating men: Leconte's use of actors

Male stars are used in two principal, definable ways in Leconte's work, ways that may at first sight appear somewhat incompatible. Firstly, Leconte repeatedly casts certain actors in roles which function as centres of consciousness and subjectivity in the filmic narrative. This suggests the assumption of a directorial alter ego, such that a model of 'Lecontian masculinity' becomes recognizable. Jean Rochefort is the most obvious example of this strategy. To date, Rochefort has starred in four of Leconte's films (*Les Vécés étaient fermés de l'intérieur, Tandem, Le Mari de la coiffeuse* and *L'Homme du train*) and has made appearances in two others (*Tango* and *Ridicule*). In several of these films, Leconte's close alignment with Rochefort is obvious. Regarding *Le Mari de la coiffeuse*, the most confessedly autobiographical of Leconte's films, the director writes: 'Comme Flaubert qui disait: "Madame Bovary c'est moi!", je n'ai pas peur de dire que je suis le mari de la coiffeuse'[14] (Leconte 2000: 200). In each of Rochefort's performances as onscreen directorial alter ego, the character he plays exploits the peculiarities of his physiognomy and physicality, especially – to quote Leconte – his 'regard de chien battu' (Leconte 2000: 86) and 'son apparence d'homme tranquille, de citoyen paisible, [...] de gentleman anglais attendant son thé ou sa partie de cricket'[15] (Leconte 2000: 86, 170–1).

The traditional onscreen directorial representative functions for the director as a masquerade of masculinity, a perfect macho hard man, who is not only an alter ego but an ego ideal. This star, then, works as both a figure of identification and as an aspirational figure, for the director and for the (male) spectator. So, although not over-

14 'Like Flaubert, who declared "Madame Bovary is me!", I am not afraid to say that I am the hairdresser's husband'

15 'hang-dog expression'; 'his appearance of a calm man, a peaceable citizen, an English gentleman awaiting his tea or his cricket match'

coming the cinematic tradition in which a male director projects an onscreen directorial alter ego, Leconte subtly subverts the meaning and ideology of the strategy, by choosing a fragile pathos-evoking protagonist to stand in his place, a figure whose persona (a combination of diegetic character and offscreen reputation) suggests mental instability or fragility (*Tandem*), loss and melancholy (*Le Mari de la coiffeuse*) and, in most recent years, the frailty of ill health and encroaching old age (*L'Homme du train*).

The projection of an alter ego in conventional narrative cinema can be read as a way of masking fears of fragmentation. In placing Rochefort, rather than some glamorous or macho figure, as the directorial alter ego, Leconte admits an awareness of the constructedness of cinematic masculinity and the fragility of the masquerade into his filmmaking with the very gesture that usually masks and disavows them. Rochefort is a self-deprecating alter ego, whose incarnations dissipate rather than shore up *auteur*ist narcissism. 'Lecontian masculinity', then, is a construction that avows, rather than smoothes out, the contradictions and imperfections of a human condition normally masked by cinematic glamour.

The second definable way in which Leconte can be said to use actors to signify models of masculinity is by casting individuals with established star images against type. Casting against type can denaturalize the relationship between the physical actor and the onscreen role. This relationship is problematic, as it tends to lead to complacent beliefs about the possibility of representing mimetically the 'reality' of consistent and unproblematic gendered identity. Thus the disruption of the actor-character self-sameness has larger implications for considerations of the inevitability of certain associations of identity (e.g. the set of associations that pass as naturally and inevitably linked rather than socially constructed: maleness, masculinity, activity, virility, machismo). The effectiveness of this strategy can be seen in the case of *Tandem*, in which Gérard Jugnot, shorn of his trademark moustache, as well as dispossessed of his 'côté beauf' and his 'voix perchée qui fait rire'[16] (France 1987), is re-presented to an audience of French comedy fans in a muted, sympathetic guise which makes him – in the director's words – 'méconnaissable'[17]

16 'loutish side'; 'laughable falsetto voice'
17 'unrecognizable'

(France 1987). By suspending the spectator's ability to recognize and anticipate the nature of the character by reference to their familiarity with the truculent comic actor, Leconte invites a reconsideration of the inevitability of assumptions of consistent or natural identity within the filmic (and, by extension, extra filmic) sphere. We might conclude from this, then, that Leconte can allow Rochefort to signify 'in character' in *Tandem*, precisely because of his constant juxtaposition in the film with a Jugnot whose persona has been so strikingly destabilized.

While the two strategies I have just described may at first glance appear incompatible (the former apparently working within an ideology of fixed identity signification; the second working to disrupt myths of identity), it can in fact be argued that Leconte puts these two strategic uses of actors into the service of the same aim: the revelation of the masculine masquerade. This is done by undermining the habitual ego-centrism of the first strategy, and by having that strategy co-exist with the second (in the persons of Rochefort and Jugnot in the microcosmic case of *Tandem*, as well as across individual filmic texts within the broader context of the whole Lecontian *œuvre*).

A particular and most striking example of this casting against type, which I have explicated with reference to Jugnot above, is the case of Belmondo and Delon in *Une chance sur deux*, a film which deliberately plays with and subverts the signification of these icons of French cinema. The discussion of 'stars' in the context of Leconte's cinema suggests inevitably a further field of enquiry: the ambivalent relationship that French cinema culture enjoys with the Hollywood tradition that created the concept of the 'star system'. In addition, it raises the related question of the nature of French perceptions of 'Americanness' in the late-twentieth century. Through its manipulations of themes of national as well as gender identity, *Une chance sur deux* offers an account of imaginary models of specifically French masculinity in the age of encroaching globalization, as I shall explore in detail below.

## L'Amour à la papa

In his commercially and critically unsuccessful exploration of uncertain paternity, *Une chance sur deux*, Leconte reunited two icons of French cinema, Belmondo and Delon, 30 years after the heyday of their popularity. This slightly plotted film is somewhat clichéd in its casting of Paradis, the Lolita of French cinema, as Alice, a wayward young woman in search of her father,[18] and in its filming of the classic devices of the action movie: suspense, explosive combat and the eventual daring rescue of the hapless female. The film's principal interest, then, lies rather in the ways in which Leconte manipulates the meanings that had accrued to Belmondo and Delon in the French 'star system' in order to problematize perceptions of masculinity at the turn of the twenty-first century.

Having initially made their names in art films of the early 1960s, both Belmondo and Delon went on to achieve the status of popular cinematic icons via their appearance in the films of the fetishist *polar* genre. Directed by such names as Henri Verneuil, José Giovanni and Jacques Deray, these films functioned somewhat like the Hollywood star system, which establishes and exploits the meanings of the star personae of given actors. The star-texts accrue their significance across a body of films, and come eventually to signify independently of any given film or role. In the context of the French cinema industry, which is not based on a studio system, this phenomenon is less developed (see Vincendeau 2000). Prior to the success of Delon and Belmondo, the label 'mainstream French star' had only really applied to *polar* actors Jean Gabin and Eddie Constantine (Forbes 1992: 53–4).

At first associated with trademark fetish props such as the trench coat and the hat, Delon's star image became more subtly defined following his success in Melville's *Le Samourai* (1967) and *Le Cercle rouge* (1970), by reference to a strict code of honour, a glacial physical appearance and psychological complexity (Forbes 1992: 55). In contrast, Belmondo's star image relied on a muscular, aggressive sexual energy and a quality of physical self-awareness. Whatever the differences between their star personae, Delon and Belmondo shared two principal characteristics in their *polar* incarnations. The first was a pose of anti-heroic solitude and self-sufficiency; the second a striking appearance of male beauty. As Ginette Vincendeau puts it, the two stars were exceptional in the 1960s as they 'put the *eroticized* male face [Delon] and male body [Belmondo] at the centre of the frame' (Vincendeau 2000: 183).

18 Leconte's casting of Paradis as a motherless daughter in search of her father's identity references her earlier appearance in *Élisa* (Jean Becker 1995) in a very similar role.

In *Une chance sur deux*, Leconte undermines the notion of the self-contained criminal hero by casting the pair as somewhat bumbling, if well-preserved, retired conmen who are unwittingly dragged back into the gun-wielding role by the shenanigans of their erstwhile 'daughter'. Moreover, the actors have changed status in this film from beautiful young male objects of desire, reconciling that uneasy cinematic antithesis of object of the gaze and action hero (Vincendeau 2000: 174), to oedipal fathers. The generational divide is emphasized in the fact that the gang of Russian Mafia criminals in the film are played by attractive, chiselled-cheek-boned young men, who suggest the physical typology of Delon's younger incarnation. References in the dialogue to the pair's previous cinematic incarnations and, particularly, the reprisal of the musical score from *Borsalino*, the film which first united them on screen in 1969, add to the nostalgic feel of the tribute movie. By focusing so baldly on the ageing process of France's most glamorous young men, Leconte invites reflection more broadly upon a waning model of French masculinity.

If star images function as recognizable archetypes of certain modes of national and gender identity, then deliberate casting against type can signify more broadly, beyond a given filmic text, as a way of undermining belief in the fixed meaning of identities. Delon and Belmondo are cast, to some extent, in each other's 'naturalized' roles in this film. Belmondo is the more anxious of the two parents, experiencing a 'crise de nerfs'[19] as he waits for Alice to return from the disco and suffering physical indisposition at moments of particular suspense. He comments, as the two men sit smoking pipes, 'nous avons l'air d'être son papa et sa maman', to which Delon responds 'tu serais sa maman'.[20]

Belmondo's character is also the one most open to the flexibility of the meanings of gender. He lets Alice drive his prized racing car, despite Delon's warnings that she doesn't have the right set of 'chromosomes' to do so, and concedes that having a daughter is just as good as he imagined having a son would be. By casting the more 'macho' Belmondo as the father with the broader and deeper emotional range, Leconte denaturalises the assumption that physical appearance and outward performance of gender are innately, causally linked to a set of emotional and sexual behavioural traits. The same is

19 'nervous crisis'
20 'we are acting like her mummy and daddy'; 'well you would be her mummy'

true, to some extent, for the less well-developed character of Alice, who is a tomboy in her choice of pastimes only, her appearance revealing a carefully constructed and stereotypical feminine beauty, right down to her dyed blonde roots. In this dislocation of appearance from performance, attitude and behaviour, Leconte's work gestures here, however modestly, towards the deconstructive gender theory of Judith Butler who argues precisely that epistemologies which naturalize as inevitable the link between gendered appearance and types of desire/behaviour, and draw knowledge from the purported link, are factitious and dangerous.[21]

In some scenes, gender trouble is conflated with an implicit address to the unstable status of national identities. In one scene, Paradis distracts a corrupt casino boss by serenading him with 'Happy Birthday' in Russian. The sexually provocative way in which she delivers her song recalls irresistibly Marilyn Monroe's tribute to Kennedy, an effect compounded by her dyed blonde hair. However, this is where the similarity ends. She is dressed in a black tuxedo, wearing dark, heavy eye make-up, and her hair is not wavy and flowing, but scraped severely back. In appearance she resembles the lesbian icon Marlene Dietrich in *Der Blaue Engel/The Blue Angel* (von Sternberg 1930), much more than Monroe. Just as the allusion to an American president is subverted by the Russian language, so the codification of femininity is complicated. Performance, dress and post-cold-war meanings of nationality blur suggesting that the possibility of interpreting identity is far from straightforward.

At other moments, the film suggests that the progressive reconfiguration of the global landscape at the turn of the century is not so much a rich field of semantic flux as a political and cultural problem for a French audience. In one scene, Alice takes her fathers into a McDonalds fast food restaurant, that supreme emblem of the domination of globalization. The themes of changing family structures and the hybridization of French culture are made to work together in this scene, as the trio is shown surrounded by single parents with their children, engaged in that most popular of 'access day' activities, regardless of the country they are in: a trip to 'MacDo'. Disconcerted by the menu, both 'fathers' defer to their 'daughter' who orders them

21 'there are no direct expressive or causal links between sex, gender, gender presentation, sexual practice, fantasy and sexuality. None of these terms captures or determines the rest' (Butler 1993b: 315).

a 'coca "light"'. The bemused repetition of this Anglicism signals a symptom of the larger issue of unwelcome cultural change, recalling the controversial 'loi Toubon' (1994), a piece of legislation designed to prevent such borrowed neologisms 'infecting' the French language.[22] The older generation, represented by Belmondo and Delon, is shown to be uncomfortable and unfamiliar with the menu's tortuous Anglicisms, while Paradis's character seems perfectly at home in Americanized France. This is particularly ironic, as Belmondo's and Delon's star images have been criticized for being too American. Pierre Maillot, for example, suggests that in the 1960s Delon's and Belmondo's onscreen incarnations of *polar* heroes glorified an American way of life and thereby represented the 'dissolution' of French national identity (Maillot 1996: 174).

Thus, in *Une chance sur deux*, it is by playing to some extent on the established meanings of the star texts Belmondo and Delon that Leconte reflects the way in which perceptions of masculinity in France are progressively destabilized. The two stars, perhaps more than any others in French cinema culture, connote both the chic Frenchness of the New Wave and yet also the sheen of Hollywood, acquired by their association with the *polar* genre. By casting these chic heroes of *noir* thrillers in a film whose generic pretensions reconcile – somewhat uneasily – action thriller and domestic comedy, by focusing on their advanced age, on the nervous disposition of the character played by the notoriously 'macho' Belmondo, and on the feminization of both actors' images, Leconte's film signifies as more than a rather thinly plotted, affectionate homage to two of his favourite actors. It demonstrates how the notion of a unitary and exemplary French masculinity of earlier decades, even if already touched with Hollywood ambition, has now segued into a more fluid and indeterminate imaginary construction involving both a 'feminization' of male emotional range and a sometimes troubling, sometimes empowering awareness of the effects of globalization. In *Une chance sur deux*, the flawless mask of French masculinity and the dual face of French patriarchy/patrimony are revealed as mythic constructions belonging to the consciousness of a cinematic and socio-political past.

Aside from its deconstruction of national masculinities, then, the film is set up to reveal one further – and related – area of deceptively

22  See: www.aacc.fr/juridique/toubon.htm.

naturalized identity: fatherhood. The theme of fatherhood is not an incidental choice in a film reflecting on fin-de-millennial masculinity. From the very beginning, there is a focus on the discourse pertaining to the valuable social role played by the benevolent patriarch. In the opening sequences we are introduced to Paradis's character Alice, a 20-year-old car thief whose manner suggests a rebellious teenager rather than a young adult woman. She is released from custody following an interview with a male official who admonishingly questions why she can't be more like his own daughter: interested in astrology and cooking; in short, 'plus normale'. Her response says it all: 'Je n'ai pas de père'.[23]

The reactionary politics set up in this initial encounter seems, on some level, to persist throughout the film. Her erratic behaviour and predilection for trouble – culminating in her being buried up to her neck in sand by a gang of criminals – suggest that she badly needs a father figure to set her on the straight and narrow. Despite her taste for masculine pursuits (cars and danger), Paradis is kept locked in the stereotype of daughterly femininity in her constant need for affirmation and rescue by the older males. However, the rhetoric of the helpless daughter is, at least, in the service of a demystifying agenda. The irony and comedy of the film's narrative logic is that these father figures – while both wanting badly to be proved to be Alice's biological parent – lack any notion of what fatherhood might mean beyond clichés and stereotypes (Belmondo always wanted a child to share his passion for cars). The two men, both powerful and rich, battle for the affection and attention of their 'daughter', each proffering a series of ever more elaborate treats and slighting the attempts of the other 'father'. The societal demand for infallible father figures and the cultural myth of the monolithic male hero are therefore debunked, as Delon and Belmondo are revealed as dysfunctional – if well meaning – fathers, and as reluctant action heroes.

Paternity is revealed in the film to be as performative as gender. Fatherhood becomes something you *do*, not something you *are* in the narrative logic. While remaining ignorant of the truth of Alice's biological paternity, both men continue to *feel like* her father, having fought so hard to occupy the role that a father plays. Judith Butler has drawn attention to the bizarre logic of the popular song's lyrics: 'You make

23 'more normal'; 'I have no father'

me feel like a natural woman'. The notion that a natural woman exists, and that ordinary (presumably artificial?) women should want to *feel like* this paeon of idealized femininity is a nonsense of commonplace ontology. The two fathers in this deceptively slight comedy, then, might metaphorically sing to Alice: 'You make me feel like a natural father'. Such a statement has particular resonance for a French film of the late 1990s that pivots around the uncertainty of being named as father. The extent of the French cultural obsession with the meaning of the name of the father came to light in the wake of a recent legal decision (2002) regarding the automatic bestowing of direct paternal patronyms on children. No longer obliged to name a child after its biological father, parents can now choose to pass on the mother's name instead, or to give the child both the mother's and the father's names, effectively fragmenting the traditional symbolic role of the father as bestower of both name and law (see Nobus 2002). Certain Lacanian psychoanalysts commenting on this social development, as well as on neighbouring phenomena such as same-sex parenting, have predicted that wide-ranging psychical consequences, equating to a mass psychotic splintering, may result from the ensuing rupture in the symbolic law (Verhaeghe 2000, Winter 2000). Such an extreme reaction suggests the dual fragility and omnipotence that the paternal role connotes within French culture. The suggestion that fatherhood may be a fragile and performative construct with culturally contingent significance, rather than an immutable given, reveals the amusing rivalrous posturing of the two 'fake' fathers of *Une chance sur deux* as another face of the hysterical masquerade of masculinity, struggling to shore up the meaning of phallic authority in a changing symbolic system.

## Some concluding remarks

In an analysis of *film noir* which would be equally pertinent to the other masculine genres discussed in this chapter, Richard Dyer argues that:

> Masculinity and normality [...] constitute the films' 'problematic', that set of issues and questions that the films seek to come to terms with without ever actually articulating. (To articulate them would already be to confront masculinity and normality as problems, whereas ideology functions on the assumption that they can be taken for granted). (Dyer 1978: 91)

The point Dyer is making in this suggestive extract has far-reaching implications. The concept 'masculinity', like 'normality', enjoys a privileged status in Western thought. It has historically appeared under erasure, as a category that does not need to be interrogated or analysed, precisely because it is taken already to connote neutrality and objectivity. Ideology functions by masking the conditions in which categories are constructed, and thereby making those categories appear 'natural'.

Dyer shows up the possibility that existing aesthetic forms and conventions, such as the filmic genre of the *noir*, may already problematize ideologically sacred 'givens' such as masculinity, but only in a partial or subtextual way, since such a questioning is always already conditioned by ideology as invalid and unthinkable. Thus, the task of demystification falls to the cultural critic. My argument in this chapter has been that Leconte's films about men expose and interrogate the commonplace myths of cinematic masculinity by bringing to the surface of the diegesis what is ordinarily subtextual in the genres in question. Leconte uses techniques of parody, dislocation, literalization and the manipulation of star personae to show up the very ideological underpinnings of the modes of cinema he both works in and comments on.

Leconte's consistent questioning of models of masculinity in European variants of Hollywood genres cannot be understood in a contextual vacuum. It is widely accepted in French cultural criticism that the 1970s and 1980s witnessed a broader 'crisis of masculinity' in France, which was prominently represented in the filmmaking of the time. The aftermath of May '68 and the concomitant rise of political feminism produced a swathe of films which highlight – somewhat ambivalently – a shift in perception regarding the meaning of gender roles. Echoing Dyer's assertion that masculinity (rather than femininity, as is usually assumed) is the silenced enigma at the core of the 1940s American *noir*, critics including Jill Forbes have highlighted masculinity as the – unacknowledged – subject matter *par excellence* of 1970s French filmmaking (Forbes 1992: 183).

Films of the 1970s explore the perceived crisis of masculinity, either by pointing up the failure of the sexual revolution to liberate men and women from bourgeois constraints (Blier) or by making the spectator aware of the ways in which existing models of male friendship and solidarity are eroded by historical and socio-economic conditions, as in the nostalgic films of Claude Sautet. For Sautet, the increased focus on individual wealth that is a symptom of accelerating capitalism led to a dissolution of the ties of collectivity that characterized the 1950s in France (Forbes 1992: 184).

If this is true of the 1970s, then it is perhaps even more the case for the hard-nosed 1980s. The subtitle of Phil Powrie's recent book on 1980s cinema, *Nostalgia and the Crisis of Masculinity* (1997), suggests that the crisis of the 1970s was not so much a discreet phenomenon as the start of a larger trend.[24] Discussing the changing status of men in this decade, Yvonne Tasker has argued that 1980s men were 'targeted as consumers of lifestyle' for the first time. This invitation to men to occupy the hitherto feminine role of consumer, rather than the masculine roles of producer or owner of the means of production (depending on class), purportedly led to a 'stress on the fabrication of identity' and 'a denaturalizing of the supposed naturalness of male identity' (Tasker 1993: 110). Tasker's assertions partially account for the increased awareness demonstrated in Leconte's films of the 1980s and 1990s of what I have been delineating the 'masculine masquerade.' In this context, it would constitute a harking back to pre-existing models of heroic or macho masculinity in order to obviate the cultural lure to lapse into the feminine position of consumer, complacently alienated from action by the comfort of luxury goods.

However, while it is both possible and helpful to refer to these broader historical-cultural factors in order to contextualize and better understand Leconte's gendered agenda, when considering the specificities of Leconte's representations, we cannot fail to see that he all

24 However, one must be careful about assumptions regarding the first instance of a crisis of masculinity in France. The end of the nineteenth century in Europe, for example, saw a fearful male reaction to the phenomenon of the 'new woman', as evidenced by the doom-laden prophecies of degeneration theory in Germany, France and Italy. Elisabeth Badinter asserts that there is inevitably a crisis afflicting fixed notions of the masculine at those moments in history when women achieve increased independence or improved status (1994a: 33). She cites examples as historically remote as seventeenth-century France and England. Finally, as Dyer would no doubt point out, masculinity, like any other constructed identity category, is perpetually subject to fluctuation, even if articulation of this fluctuation has been ideologically foreclosed. Indeed, one can argue, if the constructed nature of masculinity had not historically functioned as an unspoken secret, the notion of a 'crisis' in this identity would have no meaning.

but debars from his filmic universe the specificity of socio-political comment. His male characters in the films I have explored above are long-standing cultural and cinematic archetypes re-presented in such a way as to reveal the flaws and gaps in their own fictitious construction. In the figure of actor Jean Rochefort in particular, Leconte shows up the fragile human being negotiating the demands of the masculine masquerade. In this, Leconte abstracts from the cultural particular (socio-economic factors in France) to the philosophical abstract, and from gender to ontology.

Leconte's cinematography speaks an awareness of the constructedness of identity. As Yvonne Tasker has shown, this awareness is conditioned by and dependent upon the particularities of given social moments. While *Une chance sur deux* references such factors as the perceived cultural domination of France by America quite explicitly, in earlier films such as *Les Spécialistes*, *Tandem* and *Tango*, specific signifiers of the cultural-historical moment recede to the level of the unspoken, and the postmodern subject in his tragi-comic project of self-deconstruction occupies centre-stage. The themes of ageing and becoming symbolically impotent in these films (particularly in *Tandem*, seen in the decline of a radio career and a concomitant decline in mental stability) function on two levels. Firstly, they signify the microcosmic perceived fate of French masculinity in a changing economic climate. Secondly, they alert the viewer to the macrocosmic concern that in a postindustrial, technological and hyper-consumerist age, human beings become redundant and human life is essentially rendered meaningless. (It is significant that having lost his job, and therefore his 'identity', Mortez comforts himself at the film's close by buying a new car).

It is not my intention to assert that the films under study in this chapter qualify Leconte as a thoroughly postmodern filmmaker. Postmodern cinema in its purest form is typified by *avant-garde* experiments, such as the films of Laura Mulvey and Peter Wollen, which refuse viewing pleasure, subvert rules of unitary characterization and overcome the convention of linear narrative. Linear narrative and consistent characterization do feature in Leconte's films; however, they are presented as subject to a process of ongoing fragmentation and deconstruction.

Some other key signifiers of a postmodern cinematic mode are the effacement of the distinction between high and low culture and a proliferation of citations from other cinemas and art forms, not in order to reference their cultural context or meaning, but merely to recycle (Forbes 1992: 63). In such films as *Tango* the function of quotations from other filmmakers (Hitchcock, Buñuel, Blier) lies somewhere between parody (the modern mode) and pastiche (postmodernity). The references are in the service of a subversive point: to destabilize the naturalized misogyny that Leconte is treating. They can therefore be delineated as ethical rather than aesthetic, and said to belong to an epistemological agenda. The rhetorical strategy of misogyny (the dehumanization of women) is explored – and exposed – in Leconte's films as a defensive, projective-identificatory mechanism between men, in the face of the breakdown in traditional modes of identity and the failure of relatedness in the conventional institution of coupledom.

Where Leconte's films touch most closely – and most fruitfully – on the concerns of postmodernism is in their treatment of subjectivity. Without adopting wholly postmodern form, these films mark the awareness of a transition from one philosophical mode to another. The buddy movie, the thriller and the western, in their conventional manifestations, describe worldviews that can be delineated as existential. These filmic genres promote a belief in the possibility of creating meaning through the action, self-determination and individual will of a central character. The performance of masculinity is naturalized in such modes, rather than revealed as a contingent construction of cultural meaning-making practices. Leconte replaces this with an unstable, fragile male subject whose only possibility of creating or sustaining meaning comes through a series of repetitive performances designed to shore up certain codes of individual masculinity. Adorno has demonstrated that the masquerade of individualism that is a by-product of high capitalism is directly proportional to the 'liquidation of the individual' (Adorno 1978: 280). In exploring fragmented and ambivalent performances of the roles of 'the criminal', 'the worker', 'the heterosexual man', 'the celebrity' or 'the father', Leconte demonstrates that these categories constitute a series of masculine masquerades that compensate for a fundamental fear: the threat of human impotence and meaninglessness in the face of the move from the gendered and national certainties of modern life to the ontological instability of a postindustrial world.

## References

Adorno, Theodor (1978), 'On the Fetish-character in Music and the Regression of Listening', in Andrew Arato and Eike Gebhardt (eds), *The Essential Frankfurt School Reader*, Oxford, Blackwell, 270–99.

Austin, Guy (1996), *Contemporary French Cinema: An Introduction*, Manchester, Manchester University Press.

Badinter, Elizabeth (1994a), 'La Crise de l'identité masculine', *Sciences humaines*, 42, 32–4.

Badinter, Elizabeth (1994b), *XY: De l'identité masculine*, Paris, Livre de poche.

Butler, Judith (1993a), 'Imitation and Gender Insubordination', in Henry Abelove, Michèle Aina Barale and David M. Halperin (eds), *The Lesbian and Gay Studies Reader*, New York and London, Routledge, 307–20.

Butler, Judith (1993b), *Bodies that Matter: On the Discursive Limits of Sex*, New York and London, Routledge.

Doane, Mary Ann (1982), 'Film and the Masquerade: Theorising the Female Spectator', *Screen*, 23: 3–4, 74–87.

Doane, Mary Ann (1988), 'Masquerade Reconsidered: Further Thoughts on the Female Spectator', *Discourse*, 11: 1, 42–53.

Dyer, Richard (1978), 'Resistance through Charisma: Rita Hayworth and Gilda', in E. Ann Kaplan (ed.), *Women in Film Noir*, London, BFI, 91–9.

Forbes, Jill (1992), *The Cinema in France after the New Wave*, Basingstoke and London, Macmillan.

France, Francine (1997), 'Leconte préfère la bicyclette', *Le Matin*, 17 June.

*France Soir* (1985) 'Triomphe des *Spécialistes* dès le premier jour', 15 March.

Fuchs, Cynthia J. (1993), 'The Buddy Politic', in Steve Cohan and Ina Rae Hark (eds), *Screening the Male: Exploring Masculinities in Hollywood Cinema*, London and New York, Routledge, 192–210.

Harris, Sue (2001), *Bertrand Blier*, Manchester, Manchester University Press.

Homlund, Chris (1993), 'Masculinity as Multiple Masquerade: The "Mature" Stallone and the Stallone Clone', in Steve Cohan and Ina Rae Hark (eds), *Screening the Male: Exploring Masculinities in Hollywood Cinema*, London and New York, Routledge, 213–31.

Lacan, Jacques ([1958] 1966), 'La Signification du phallus', in *Ecrits*, Paris, Seuil, 685–95.

Leconte, Patrice (2000), *Je suis un imposteur*, Paris, Flammarion.

Maillot, Pierre (1996), *Les Fiancés de Marianne: la société française à travers ses grands acteurs*, Paris, Le Cerf.

Modleski, Tania ([1988] 1989), *The Women Who Knew Too Much: Hitchcock and Feminist Theory*, London and New York, Routledge.

Nobus, Dany (2002), 'Symptom and Society: A Clinical Challenge for Contemporary Psychoanalysis', *Modern Psychoanalysis*, 27: 2, 179–203.

Powrie, Phil (1997), *French Cinema in the 1980s: Nostalgia and the Crisis of Masculinity*, Oxford, Oxford University Press.

Rivière, Joan (1929), 'Womanliness as a Masquerade', *The International Journal of Psychoanalysis*, 10, 303–13.

Samuels, Robert (1998), *Hitchcock's Bi-textuality: Lacan, Feminisms and Queer Theory*, Albany, State University of New York Press.

Sedgwick, Eve Kosofsky (1985), *Between Men: English Literature and Homo-sexual Desire*, New York, Columbia University Press.

Sineux, Michel (1987), 'Tandem: L'auto(im)mobile', *Positif*, September, 64–5.

Tasker, Yvonne (1993), *Spectacular Bodies: Gender, Genre and the Action Cinema*, New York and London, Routledge.

Verhaeghe, Paul (2000), 'The Collapse of the Function of the Father and its Effect on Gender Roles', in Renata Salecl (ed.), *Sexuation*, Durham NC, Duke University Press, 131–54.

Vincendeau, Ginette (1992), 'The Fathers and Daughters of French Cinema', *Sight and Sound*, March 14–17.

Vincendeau, Ginette (2000), *Stars and Stardom in French Cinema*, London, Continuum.

Winter, Jean-Pierre (2000), 'Gare aux enfants symboliquement modifiés', *Le Monde des débats*, March, 18.

Wyatt, Justin (2001), 'Identity, Queerness and Homosocial Bonding: The Case of Swingers', in Peter Lehman (ed.), *Masculinity: Bodies, Movies, Culture*, New York and London, Routledge, 51–66.

# 4

# Visions of femininity

> Lo! in yon brilliant window niche
> How statue-like I see thee stand,
> The agate lamp within thy hand!
> 'To Helen', Edgar Allan Poe

Leconte is a filmmaker who has been accused of looking too much and too hard at the female figure. This criticism is levelled particularly at three controversial films, *Monsieur Hire*, *Le Mari de la coiffeuse* and *Le Parfum d'Yvonne*. In an article on cinematic voyeurism, Geoff Andrew defines *Monsieur Hire* as the politically problematic story of a sexually immature male voyeur and a female object of the gaze who, the film implies, is inappropriately 'flattered' by the voyeur's attentions (Andrew 1990: 37). Regarding *Le Mari de la coiffeuse*, Guy Austin has written that although 'a woman [...] may form the ostensible focus of the *récit*', it is only as fetishized object and not as a 'discrete individual' with the ability to narrate her own story (Austin 1996: 55). And, in a particularly acidic review of *Le Parfum d'Yvonne*, Martin Bright describes Leconte's worldview as glimpsed in that film as 'creepy' and 'deeply sick'. He justifies the use of these adjectives by reference to Leconte's tendency to exploit both the '"Gallic" combination of love and death' and ostentatiously fetishistic camera work: 'Leconte finds plenty of excuses for sticking his camera up Sandra Majani's skirt – he doesn't need one of the characters to be looking that way either' (Bright 1994: 44).

In different ways, then, the three films in question seem to be intimately concerned with the gaze, incorporating the spectacle of the female body as part of their thematic and formal core. They can be argued to constitute either symptoms of the director's personal voyeuristic vision (as suggested by Bright in the citation above), or else as a tripartite self-referential reflection on the mechanisms of cinematic voyeurism. Where the dividing line falls between these two – ideologically very distinct – projects of representation, however, is extremely difficult to define. In this chapter, I will attempt the knotty task of evaluating Leconte's three films in the light of this critical conundrum. This will involve, firstly, a rehearsal of the principal theoretical assumptions guiding discussions of fetishistic voyeurism in the cinema, and secondly, a rigorous close reading of the films in order to expose the broader narrative logics in which their allegedly sexist spectacles are embedded. For reasons that will become clear in the course of my argument, I will consider the three films in counter-chronological order.

## Regarding the gaze

Voyeurism and fetishism are concepts with considerable critical currency in film studies. In 1975, Christian Metz theorized that film, in contradistinction to theatre, which admits of the possibility of actor–audience interaction, is an inherently voyeuristic art form. The cinema-goer is immobile, plunged into darkness and, in this self-enclosed, subjective state, requires only 'that the actor should behave as though he were not seen (and therefore as though he did not see his voyeur)' (Metz [1975] 1985: 547).

Metz's theory of the peculiarly hermetic subject/object nature of cinematic spectatorship was harnessed in the gender-specific account offered by psychoanalytically informed feminist work undertaken in the 1970s. The most influential of such accounts is undoubtedly Laura Mulvey's canonical *Screen* article of 1975, 'Visual Pleasure and Narrative Cinema'. The stark logic she draws in this piece can be paraphrased as follows: a man is gazing at a beautiful woman and desiring her; the woman is fixed as his object; denuded of subjectivity, unable to look back. All men (actor, viewer, director) are interchangeable with this man; all women (whether in the audience or on the screen – it is assumed she will not be behind the camera) are interchangeable with this woman. Looking is not politically or sexually neutral in this model; rather the cinematic apparatus mirrors the patriarchal law that constitutes the woman as a castrated fetish object of the gaze. The spectatorial role is then, by definition, a masculine one according to this argument, such that any woman spectator enjoying a cinematic spectacle finds herself occupying a position of 'bad faith'.

As fetishism is such a key concept in gaze theory, it is worth rehearsing its origins here. According to Sigmund Freud's influential account (1927), fetishism occurs when the boy child cannot admit to consciousness the difference between the sexes: the fact that women have no penis. In Freud's theory of the Oedipus complex, the child desires his mother and fears retribution from his father. Discovery of the genital differences between the sexes leads the boy to the assumption that his mother must have been castrated (that she has lost her penis). This revelation convinces the boy that he too could be punished in the same way. By creating a fetish (an object that he can invest with meaning and sexual interest that stands in place of the mother's lost phallus), the boy is able to disavow his mother's castration: 'he has retained that belief, but he has also given it up' (Freud [1927] 1991: 353). In cinematic terms, the glittering object that is the body of the female actress serves simultaneously to arouse desire and anxiety and to stand in place of the fearful absence that is the gaping wound of female sexual difference. Fetishism in the cinema, then, is not an unequivocal matter of pleasure for the masculine spectator.

Although 'Visual Pleasure and Narrative Cinema' continues to function as an obligatory reference point for any discussion of desirous beholding in the cinema, Mulvey herself (1981) and others have subsequently nuanced the terms of the original argument, suggesting, for example, that the male spectator's position may be masochistic rather than sadistic (Studlar 1988), and that certain cinematic genres encourage male spectatorial identification with female onscreen characters (Clover 1992). Moreover, in the late 1980s and 1990s, the insights of gender studies and queer theory, inspired by names such as Judith Butler, have helped to mobilize the meanings attributed to gendered and sexed identities. Queer spectatorship theorizes a fluid, plural series of partial identifications that are not inevitably tied to the sex/gender of the onscreen object or the viewer. Under the sway of queer theory, then, the gaze is freed up from the notion of castration anxiety and the inevitable phallic logic of spectatorship is obviated.

My exploration of Leconte's filmic representations will attempt to establish the extent to which he can be said to treat the filming of women's bodies in such a way that watching is not linear, phallic and fetishistic but open to interpretations that are undermining, ludic or admitting of plural types of pleasure and subjectivity. The question in hand then: does Leconte film the woman in the manner of a fetishist, operating under the sway of disavowal and seeking to retain the imaginary phallic sheen of the eternal feminine? Or does he attempt to unmask disavowal; to show that the masculine fantasy underpinning representation of the woman is no more than that: a subjective fantasy that is culturally constructed?

### Filming the fetish: *Le Parfum d'Yvonne*

The olfactory promise and suggestion of synaesthesia implicit in the title of Leconte's film are misleading in the extreme. The protagonist of *Le Parfum d'Yvonne*, Victor Chmara (Hippolyte Girardot), a deserter from the Algerian war, confines himself through the course of this 89–minute film to looking at and touching his movie star girlfriend, Yvonne (Sandra Majani), repetitively and obsessively. Close-ups on various body parts of Majani (usually her buttocks, legs and breasts) fill many frames and effectively slow down what is already a very slow and dreamy narrative, in conformity with Mulvey's account of the female fetish-body as that which fixes rather than propels action.

One of the most iconic images of the film is of Majani on the deck of a boat, leaning languorously over the railings, looking out to sea. She is wearing a white dress, head scarf and big round sunglasses, in a style reminiscent of Jackie O (figure 9). The camera moves lazily over her body, pausing on her bottom as the wind lifts her dress, revealing an arc of creamy buttock. The inclusion of this shot would at first appear to be explicable only in terms of the established theory of cinematic fetishism, an erotic display offered for the titillation of the male viewer. Such a sequence does nothing to supplement narrative development; it is static in every way except for the sinuous movement of the desiring camera. However, in the film's closing moments, the unfolding of the diegetic narrative is replaced with scenes that come from a reel of film taken using a hand-held cine-camera. The frames show Yvonne on the boat, and adumbrate the earlier spectacle filmed by Leconte. We understand, then, that this piece of film was taken by Victor with the cine-camera we have seen him use at earlier moments. The fetishism of the original sequence onboard the boat is thus displaced away from the directorial vision in these closing shots, as the image of desire is identified as Victor's and – more broadly – as it takes on the status of the 'universal' object of cinephilia.

What is the effect of this strategy? The fact that Yvonne is an actress in the world of the narrative and that this is a film *about* filming her reveals a self-reflexivity at the level of the diegesis, suggesting self-awareness on the director's part and the possibility of a reading admitting of ironic comment and parody. Yet simultaneously, and equally convincingly, it can be argued that this embedded second level of framing constitutes a narcissistic *mise en abyme*, in which fetishism of the female is the content of every level of signification at work in the film. It is notoriously difficult to locate 'scare quotes' in the realm of the visual and any exploration of this question raises inevitably the difficulty of establishing the status of authorial intention.

Using the text itself as the only means we have of establishing signification, it is possible to isolate further examples where the predominant fetishization of Yvonne's body is suddenly subject to distancing or potential undermining. In one scene, Yvonne is walking along a country road in front of Victor. The camera, suggesting alignment with his point of view, meanders after her, focusing on her back, bottom and legs. Suddenly she turns and asks him to walk in front of her. Yvonne's words, articulating and making us conscious of the spatial positioning of the male and female bodies, may cause the critically aware spectator to wonder if Leconte will reverse their respective positions at this point and align his camera with Yvonne's point of view, perhaps focusing desirously on her male lover's bottom. Instead, when Victor overtakes her, the camera remains fixed, showing only Victor's receding back. Just as the spectator assumes this to be a failure or a refusal on Leconte's part to film from the female's point of view, to acknowledge her subjectivity as well as enjoying her as object of the gaze, the camera pans round and we see that Yvonne is no longer there. In a playful gesture, she is hiding from her lover in nearby bushes. This thwarting of expectations may make us wonder whether Leconte was playing with his spectator by drawing attention to the structural cinematic absence that is the woman's desiring gaze. When he sets up the possibility of this gaze, only to then withhold it by means of a prank, the director himself seems to be engaging in a game of hide and seek. Whatever Leconte's *intention* here, the sequence is interesting for what it reveals about expectations and conventions of looking and being looked at and the potential of narrative cinema to reflect on its own limitations.

At certain moments in the film, the spectator is offered the possibility of distancing him/herself from the cloying and suffocating world depicted on the screen. In a scene that takes place in a hotel bedroom, Victor and Yvonne make love on a bed. Their hands on each other's bodies move exaggeratedly slowly and the pace and atmosphere of the scene are dreamy, suggesting an appeal to identificatory rapture. Suddenly, we cut to a shot of three budgerigars in a nearby cage. They are lined up, like spectators at an event or at the cinema, apparently watching avidly the scene on the bed. This humorous moment again draws attention to the staged nature of the erotic spectacle and causes the spectator to abandon any colluding feelings of eroticism or desire in favour of laughter.

Despite these moments of rupture, when narrative meaning seems to be temporarily mobilized and undermined, the film as a whole is conventionally narrated, by means of a male voice-over and a collection of flashbacks. Yet, this classic narrative device itself has an inbuilt twist: Victor tells his story in close up, his face lit by a soft red glow. At the end of the film, we are made aware that he is staring into the flames coming from the burnt-out car in which his friend, Dr René Meinthe (Jean-Pierre Marielle) has just committed suicide.

The figure of René Meinthe is a problematic one in numerous ways. In the book which inspired *Le Parfum d'Yvonne*, Patrick Modiano's *Villa Triste* (1975), the protagonists are several years younger than in Leconte's film. Thus, Victor and Yvonne are callow teenagers experiencing love for the first time, while Meinthe is a vigorous, luminous young gay man. Leconte's re-creation of Meinthe as a bitter and eccentric ageing homosexual, is particularly hard to read. With his flamboyant gestures and dress (gloves and a fez), 'camp' persona and depressive moods, he appears at once humorous and pathetic, offering at least a welcome antidote to the erotic banality of the heterosexual couple. Yet, the most disturbing aspect of Meinthe is the ambivalent signs of internalized homophobia he demonstrates, dismissing a brand of cigarettes as 'cigarettes pour pédés'[1] and viciously attacking a young gay man, 'La Carlton', by referring to his queen-like demeanour. This would suggest that rather than offering a queer mirror with which to question discourses of the heterosexual couple, Meinthe is primarily a figure for the internalization of homophobia.

However, his function in the film is, at least potentially, to interrupt the closed heterosexual dyad of Yvonne and Victor and to rupture the complacent fetishism of the spectacle. Meinthe's role in relation to the patterns of mobility and immobility in the film is significant. Scenes of Yvonne and Victor are characterized by the slow languor I have described above. Their listless ghostliness, as they drape themselves over divans or take up statuesque poses in beautiful gardens, is reminiscent of the characters in Resnais's *L'Année dernière à Marienbad* (1961), who argue perpetually and fruitlessly about the existence or non-existence of their affair the previous year. Meinthe provides an effective contrast with Victor's stultifying erotic self-absorption. He is associated with his car, which he likes to drive at breakneck speed, initially because 'Yvonne ... elle adore ça'[2] and finally, in the closing scenes of the film, in order to crash and kill himself. Meinthe's suicide is a semantic puzzle, suggesting both an existential bid for self-assertion outside of the cloying environment he lives in, and an articulation of the homophobic self-loathing problematically displayed by the character.

On another level, Meinthe's suicide suggests a parallel between him and Yvonne. Trapped by the codes of heterosexist representation, seen only through the eyes of Victor or the lens of cameras (Victor's and Leconte's), neither Yvonne nor Meinthe can escape the normalizing gaze. While Yvonne is put on display as a female object of desire, Meinthe's raffish, stereotyped appearance constructs him as a visible sexual anomaly, an object of fear and ridicule. Their plight is evoked by the film's leitmotif of butterflies (Victor claims that he is selling off his father's collection of rare ones to make a living). Yvonne, then, is effectively a butterfly too: beautiful to look at but pinned down, fixed in a state of immobility by the predatory gaze. She (partially) escapes Victor's attempts to possess her by running away with another man but this action is then recuperated and understood by reference to

1  'cigarettes for poofters'
2  'Yvonne loves that'

codes of feminine perfidy. Meinthe's means of escape is via another route: suicide, an act of self-determination which also signifies, however, as the inevitable punishment befalling dissident sexuality. Thus, despite his 'drive' to evade entrapment through mobility (quite literally in the speeding car), Meinthe ends as just another victim. This leaves only Victor, lonely but intact, as the speaking subject who narrates their stories.

Only occasionally do humour, irony or techniques of defamiliarization break the oneiric and onanistic fantasy surface of this film, to suggest that rather than being a superficial male fantasy, this is a film *about* male obsession with the female love object. Ultimately, then, the moments of subversion and disruption notwithstanding, this film seldom moves outside of Victor's desiring subjectivity, which, for the most part, it is hard to imagine Leconte does not take a bit too seriously. Whether Leconte's film is read as a celebration of the fetishization of the woman or as an attempt to draw this cinematic convention to our attention, may in the end be unanswerable, as its framing is conservative, attributing subjectivity and the power of narration to the heterosexual male, and ultimately failing to offer any alternative solution to the impasse in representation.

## Eros and Thanatos at the hairdressers

*Le Mari de la coiffeuse* is a *film intime*, comprising a limited *mise en scène*, a tiny cast and 'un scénario de rien du tout'[3] (Copperman 1990). It narrates the life of Antoine (Jean Rochefort) whose boyhood was coloured by his erotic attachment to Mme Schaeffer, a voluptuous hairdresser who died of an overdose of barbiturates, leaving him with an enduring obsession for female hairdressers. In adulthood, Antoine meets a worthy successor, Mathilde (Anna Galiena), whom he marries. One stormy afternoon, after a passionate session of lovemaking, Mathilde runs out into the rain and drowns herself in the swollen river. She leaves a note which reveals that she wanted their happiness to remain perfect, therefore she must die while it is at its height.

If the subject matter is bizarre but modest – the sentimental life of a death-haunted hairdresser-fetishist – the film itself functions as an

3 'a script as light as a feather'

ambitious and wide-ranging homage to certain traditions of representation (particularly literary, but also filmic) that fetishize the figure of the dead or dying woman and privilege a nostalgic, death-driven eroticism over life-driven sexuality. That this is primarily a film about remembering and repeating – both emotional experiences within the diegetic world and artistic constructions of emotion in the extra-diegetic reality – can be seen on several levels.

Firstly, the film is structured around a series of flashbacks to Antoine's boyhood and in particular to scenes of him playing on the beach at Luc-sur-mer. At one point, Antoine's 12-year-old self is reluctantly forced by his mother to wear a pair of itchy woollen bathing trunks decorated with pompoms. The embarrassing recollection has an extra-diegetic resonance, as it was inspired by an event in the director's own life concerning 'des "home made slips"' that the young Leconte was also compelled to wear (Leconte 2000: 28). The ridiculous garment with its pendulous pompoms – reminiscent of the floppy woollen cap worn by Charles in the opening pages of *Madame Bovary* – is suggestive of fragile, exposed male sex organs.[4]

This insertion of personal memories into the screenplay, and the casting of *acteur fétiche* Rochefort as protagonist, suggest that this sentimental film has particular emotional resonance for the director. However, despite the suggestiveness of the episode of the 'home made slips' for the critic of a psychoanalytical persuasion, Leconte is forceful in his repudiation of 'toute lecture de texte freudienne'[5] (Leconte 2000: 38) that might be applied to his work. Nonetheless, it is not surprising given the textbook Freudian subject matter of this film that psychoanalytic criticism has been brought to bear on *Le Mari de la coiffeuse* by academic critics.

Far from offering the crude psychobiography that the director no doubt fears, however, Paul Sutton's psychoanalytic reading of the film in a 1999 article offers a nuanced analysis of the film's peculiar melancholic-nostalgic structure. For Sutton, *Le Mari de la coiffeuse*

4 The young Charles Bovary is mocked by his school fellows in Flaubert's novel for wearing a strange hat decorated by 'une façon de sac [...] d'où pendait, au bout d'un long cordon trop mince, un petit croisillon de fils d'or en manière de gland' ('a sort of sack, from which hung, at the end of a long, excessively thin cord, a little acorn-shaped drop woven from golden thread') (Flaubert [1857] 1972: 24).

5 'any Freudian reading'

represents an example of cinematic *afterwardsness*, a term he borrows from the post-Freudian psychoanalyst Jean Laplanche who used it to translate Freud's *Nachträglichkeit*. *Afterwardsness* signifies the process by which deferred meaning and affect are activated only by a second occurrence of a meaningful event (i.e. the sexual nature of Antoine's feelings for Mme Schaeffer are only realized once he meets Mathilde). This retrospective activation of meaning is also an assumption of loss, since the presence of the second object announces the disappearance of the original object. Sutton's argument is that Mathilde is constructed as a fetish of mourning in the film – she is the object which replaces and yet constantly evokes reminders of Antoine's original lost object, Mme Schaeffer.

Yet simultaneously, claims Sutton, Mathilde is the locus of a consciousness of 'transcience', as Freud uses the term in his 1915 paper of that name. By this, Freud refers to a feeling of sorrow in the present for a loss that *will be* experienced in the future; for example, when we become aware that a flower we find beautiful will inevitably fade. In the context of the dreamy, memory-haunted framing of her relationship with Antoine, the figure of Mathilde serves to remind the watcher constantly of the loss that *will have to be endured*: the death of their passion, either by its becoming old, tired and mundane, or by the physical death that will separate them.

I am persuaded by Paul Sutton's analysis and yet find that its model of fetishism and deferral do not completely account for the structural means by which the film works upon the viewer. As well as playing with temporal sequence in the form of flashback/screen memory, the film is structured according to a series of compulsive repetitions. The ideas Freud propounds in 'On Transcience' and 'Fetishism' both predate his formulation of the controversial theory of the death drive and the life drive.[6] This speculative theory accounts for the way in which the psyche, under the sway of the death drive, is called upon to repeat painful as well as pleasurable experiences in the service of an exigency '*to restore an earlier state of things*' (Freud [1920] 1991: 331). This model suggests certain interesting implications for

6 Although 'Fetishism' (1927) was published later than *Beyond the Pleasure Principle* (1920), the text of 1927 draws on ideas developed much earlier in Freud's career and that belong to his earlier thinking. Most of the central tenets of the 1927 essay can be found in Freud's lecture of 1909, 'On the Genesis of Fetishism', which remained unpublished until 1988 (see Rose 1988).

cinema theory, as film is often structured repetitively and seeks to repair trauma by re-viewing cultural and personal memory, however painful.

The drive towards death is a thematic as well as structural feature of this film. The text is aware of its place in a lineage of representations of heterosexual love that not only end in, but are coloured and propelled by death. Guy Austin, pursuing an argument made by Naomi Segal, uses *Le Mari de la coiffeuse* to exemplify a type of French film that is structured along similar lines to the eighteenth-century genre of the French *récit* (Austin 1996: 54–7). According to Segal's analysis of this literary genre, the *récit* usually features a male narrator and a woman who ultimately dies. The woman's death provides the climax of the narrative, while the man inevitably lives on in order to tell her tale from his viewpoint (Segal 1988: 9).

In addition to the striking similarities between Leconte's film and the eighteenth-century *récit*, parallels can be drawn between *Le Mari de la coiffeuse* and certain nineteenth-century narratives which focus on female love objects who die and are resurrected as phantoms or fantasies (Théophile Gautier's 'La cafetière', Edgar Allan Poe's 'Morella' and 'Ligeia', Villiers de l'Isle-Adam's 'Véra') or whose death brings narrative closure (Flaubert's *Madame Bovary*, Zola's *Nana* (1880)). As I have argued elsewhere (Downing 2003), nineteenth-century French literature privileges a necrophiliac aesthetic, that is one in which the dying or dead object of sexual desire functions as an idealized iconic reminder of the writer/reader/narrator's own – equally desired and feared – mortality. According to this analogy, the figure of the suicidal Mathilde functions not as a figure of individual subjectivity but as an impersonal, machine-like embodiment of the principle of the death drive, that wishes 'to die only in its own fashion' (Freud [1920] 1991: 312). The woman's body in this film, then, certainly does serve as a foil for the masculine spectator, but it is not so much the threat of castration that she evokes/forestalls as a glimpse into the abyss – an abyss constructed and approximated by centuries of literary fantasy and speculation.

Literary intertexts interpenetrate this film in several ways. It is primarily a peculiarly literary film, signalled by the continuous use of voice-over, that cinematic version of the first-person narrative. Moreover, the nature of Antoine's first-person account is heavily redolent of the style and preoccupations of the French classics. The opening words of the voice-over, accompanying an image of Antoine alone, in a sombre setting, clipping his own hair, are: 'J'eus la tête encombrée de souvenirs encombrants'.[7] The tone is heavily literary, given both in the use of the *passé simple*, the French narrative tense, as opposed to the more informal spoken perfect tense, and in the poetic structure of the line, with its repetition of 'encombrer' suggesting chiasmus, a device used to create an echoing sonority within a single line of verse. Moreover, the words remind the viewer schooled in French literature of Charles Baudelaire's poem treating the weight of accumulated memory, 'Spleen', which opens: 'J'ai plus de souvenirs que si j'avais mille ans / Un gros meuble à tiroirs encombré de bilans'[8] (Baudelaire 1975: 73).

The nineteenth-century sensibility of the film hinges, then, on the preoccupation shared by writers of that period and Leconte with the poeticization of the nexus of loss and desire. However, the movement of repetition is not only understandable by reference to the emotional content and timbre of the film. The literariness of this filmic text – the way it causes the viewer to repeat collective memories and myths accrued from a shared cultural image bank – suggests an extra-diegetic repetition compulsion.

As well as referencing a historical tradition of literary representations that link the female beloved to death, *Le Mari de la coiffeuse* explores this idea with reference to a cinematic tradition. Of all his films to date, *Le Mari de la coiffeuse* probably shows the most signs of being indebted to Leconte's hero, Truffaut. Its themes of childhood reminiscence and heterosexual adolescent embarrassment recall the preoccupations of the Doinel cycle (the protagonist of *Le Mari de la coiffeuse* is also called Antoine), while Mathilde's suicide recalls a seminal *nouvelle vague* reference: the murder-suicide of Catherine (Jeanne Moreau) in Truffaut's *Jules et Jim* (1962). Critics have argued that *Jules et Jim* works to establish Catherine as a fetishized object of desire and as a representational archetype of femininity by numerous means. The most striking of these strategies is the prefiguration of the eponymous heroes' meeting with Catherine in their discovery of a statue of a woman's head that resembles Moreau. The notion of the lost original object that is later refound is thus paralleled in the statue/Catherine and the Schaeffer/Mathilde pairs.

7 'My mind was cluttered with burdensome memories'
8 'I have more memories than one who had lived for a thousand years / A large chest of drawers cluttered with documents'

It has been argued that Catherine's reckless and apparently unmotivated leap into the Seine, and her final act of murder-and-suicide by driving herself and Jim into a millpond, constitute the only possibilities of escape from the heavily codified and imprisoning representations of her as the 'eternal feminine'. While for Kathleen Murphy, Moreau's reckless leaps into the abyss create a transgressive 'moment of meaning' (Murphy 1992: 29), for Fiona Handyside, this 'moment of self-determination [...] is achieved only at the highest price'. It marks the point at which 'her possession in discourse is total. She is revealed through this action to be the *femme fatale* of cinematic convention' (Handyside 2003: 160).

The *femme fatale* is a figure with a long history. In a study of nineteenth-century Decadent representations of the figure, Bram Dijkstra (1986) has pointed to a split in the figuration of the *femme fatale*. She is either the punishing, castrating, deadly female *or* the woman whose sexuality is fatal only to herself (implicitly as a punishment for male fears and projections regarding female sexual power). Molly Haskell defines the figure of the filmic *femme fatale* as embodying both polarities: 'She is almost inevitably a male invention, the projection – and prisoner – of a director's or writer's fears and fantasies, and probably a means of satisfying his own destructive urges. In return, she is flattered by being worshipped as a goddess.' (Haskell 1997: 67). Mathilde is a *femme fatale* in only one of the senses defined by Dijkstra, and, significantly, it is as the embodiment of the nineteenth-century dying/dead beloved, rather than the killer chick of the *film noir*. Where Truffaut's Moreau embodies *both* types of fatality, straddling convention and modernity, Mathilde is fatal only to herself and disappears as easily as she came into being: as a phantom or, more accurately, a recurrent death-haunted dream.

Yet, the film contains several elements which work to prevent it becoming a wholly death-driven art work, giving itself up to the lure of the repetition compulsion and sucking the spectator into a nihilistic void of memory. The elements I am referring to are not, as may at first appear likely, the comic aspects of the narrative, since, where the film segues into comedy (e.g. the boyhood scene of Antoine's embarrassing shorts), the gags themselves are already weighted with nostalgia and pregnant with sexual innuendo. Nor am I thinking of the bizarre leitmotif of Antoine's penchant for Arab dancing. Despite their strangeness, the scenes in which the very French, very middle-aged

Rochefort undulates incongruously to the accompaniment of Eastern music can perhaps be understood as another facet of the nostalgic nineteenth-century sensibility of the film. For the Romantics and the Parnassians, the Eastern world suggested a potent exoticism and eroticism, which they reified as a facet of French aestheticism. Rather, the moments of rupture are found in the only interventions in the film that fall outside of Antoine's artillery of associations, projections and identifications, and which offer a humorous meta-narrative. I am thinking of the conversations by the clients in the hairdressing salon, in particular, the couple of garrulous old men who appear twice in the film and whose exchanges take the form of philosophical enquiries.

The first time they appear, they engage in a debate about the status of the original and the copy, with reference to flowers: 'Si'l n'y avait pas eu de naturelles d'abord, il n'y aurait pas d'artificielles main-tenant',[9] argues the first. The second counters with : 'et les moulins de café? [...] il n'y a pas de moulins de café naturels [...] mais ça ne les empêche pas d'exister'.[10] At this point in the film, Antoine is halfway through his retelling of his fascination with hairdressers. We have not yet been shown Mme Schaeffer's death, nor the circumstances of his meeting with Mathilde. The dialogue announces the link between the foundational object and Antoine's future wife, but it abstracts the link from the level of the text to a wider debate regarding the belief in the original. It is a debate dear to the heart of postmodernism, which refutes the existence of the 'original' and suggests the possibility of creativity without recourse to myths of authenticity.

The second intervention of the old men comes close to the end of the film and, appropriately enough, is on the subject of death. They discuss the proximity of death to sleep, the first man proposing: 'C'est comme quand on dort et qu'on ne rêve pas'.[11] The other counters that the possibility of waking is precisely what defines sleep. The first man then amends his definition: 'de toute façon, il n'a pas conscience'.[12] The second adds to this proposition: 'disons qu'on n'a pas conscience

9 'If there hadn't been any natural ones to start with, there wouldn't be any artificial ones now'
10 'and what about coffee mills? There are no coffee mills in nature, but that doesn't stop them existing'
11 'it's like when you sleep but don't dream'
12 'well anyway, he is not conscious'

de rien'.[13] The first man then corrects him again, drawing an abrupt distinction between 'celui qui n'a pas conscience de rien' and 'celui qui n'a pas de conscience'.[14] The first man then seeks Antoine's opinion. Rochefort's face is filmed in close-up, enigmatic and pensive for a moment before he gives his answer: 'La mort est jaune citron et sent la vanille'.[15] Unsurprisingly for one with a romantic fixation on a dead love object, Rochefort refers to death by means of an idealistic appeal to the senses. Antoine's synaesthetic, Baudelairean romanticism thus contrasts with the clients' pedantic discourse of logic. The customers' philosophical discussion about death functions, then, to remind us that the great unknowable mystery is recuperated constantly by the subject *in and as discourse*. Talking openly about discourses of death and consciousness in a film that, for the most part, repeats long-held discursive fictions about death and romanticism, points to a level of awareness outside of the seductive realm of Antoine's death-driven subjectivity that fissures the surface of this trance of a film.

These interventions, then, speak the film's awareness of its place within a tradition of representations of love that fixes romance in a lack-driven economy and the shadow of death. While endorsing the tradition and producing a cinematic vision of the female that is in conformity with the feminist critique levelled by Mulvey and others, the elements of self-reflexiveness in Leconte's film nonetheless signal a desire to rupture the fetishistic repetition compulsion that produces reactionary representations. The pain experienced while watching the film is the peculiar pain of the inevitability of loss experienced in advance of the event, signalled by Paul Sutton as transcience. However, the inevitable repetition in question is not only the fetishistic object-choice of Antoine, as representative centre of consciousness onscreen, but the repetition of certain imaginary and symbolic constructs of the fatal heterosexual romantic relationship, which originate in myths as deeply rooted in the cultural imaginary as Tristan and Isolde. This film is at once about the tension between preserving and breaking with the lost object – not only the bodies of Mme Schaeffer and Mathilde, but the meanings accrued to textual bodies through time and tradition.

13  'let's say he wouldn't be conscious of anything'
14  'he who is not aware of anything'; 'he who is without consciousness'
15  'death is the colour of lemons and has the scent of vanilla'

## *Monsieur Hire*: the multiple gaze

If Hitchcock's *Rear Window* (1954) is the best-known and most widely discussed of those films which consciously set out to address voyeurism, to be movies about watching and, by extension, 'movie[s] about watching movies' (Lemire 2000: 57), then Leconte's *Monsieur Hire* is a close contender. The similarities between *Rear Window* and *Monsieur Hire* are numerous. Both films exploit the analogy between the illuminated window and the cinema screen as loci of suspense and desire. Both feature a voyeuristic male protagonist in a state of claustrophobic confinement (physical in the case of Hitchcock's Jeff (James Stewart); emotional in the case of M. Hire (Michel Blanc)). And both, broadly, are parables about the dangers of falling in love.

However, the outcome of the sexual relationships in these two films, and the configurations of gendered power, work rather differently. In *Rear Window*, Jeff's girlfriend Lisa is so eager to please her lover and ultimately to persuade him to marry her, that she puts her own life at risk investigating the wife-murderer Thorvald, with whom Jeff is obsessed. In *Monsieur Hire*, Alice's loyalty to her murderous boyfriend Émile leads her to frame M. Hire for the killing of Pierrette Bourgeois, which in turn leads to his death. In both cases, the woman carries out an act of sacrifice for her lover; however, in *Monsieur Hire*, the victim of the sacrifice is the betrayed other rather than the self. Although motivated by love for a man, Alice in *Monsieur Hire* is not a traditional feminine filmic stereotype. She is neither just a passive object to be looked at (indeed her actions drive the plot forward and precipitate its conclusion), nor a straightforward victim. She incorporates elements of the traditional *femme fatale* of *noir* (seductiveness, danger, perfidy), but also deviates from the archetype in a number of ways (she is not 'decoded', she remains alive). Hire, the *voyeur*, is not accorded complete mastery through his gaze, and it is he rather than the *femme fatale* whose death will provide filmic closure. Thus, in its framing and characterization, the film is ambiguous and inventive.

Noting these departures from the generic norm, Abigail Murray's 1993 article 'Voyeurism in *Monsieur Hire*' proposes that Leconte's film restructures the gendered codes of voyeurism, such that '*Monsieur Hire* [...] sets up the gaze as male but only to bring into question the existing structures of looking in the cinema which are based on the active/male, passive/female dichotomy' (Murray 1993: 93). The gaze is indeed set up as male in the very early stages of the film. The credits, accompanied by a baroque score by Michael Nyman, give way to a spectacle of a dead female body lying in a field. The camera pans upwards to show a detective (André Wilms) watching the corpse intently. He then muses, via a voice-over, on the sad fate of the victim. A few frames later, we see the body lying in the morgue and the policeman taking photographs of the dead girl's face. The male gaze takes possessive mastery of this inert female in the most radical way: it immortalizes her mortality. Following this shot of the dead child, we cut to a live child, playing a game of hide and seek on the doorstep with M. Hire. Shortly after, we are offered shots of Alice (Sandrine Bonnaire), dressing to meet her boyfriend and then undressing again to make love to him, silhouetted against the light in her bedroom window. These images are seen from the point of view of Hire, who watches from the shadowy interior of the flat opposite hers. By placing sequences of the murdered body, Hire's game with the little girl, and his fascination with Alice in close proximity, Hire's voyeurism accrues associations of sinister intent. These early scenes, then, include both conventional *noir* elements (murder and the spectacle of the alluring woman) and a traditional configuration of gendered surveillance, which the director will later go on to subvert.

The subversion in question is achieved firstly by divesting the male watcher of power. The figure of M. Hire is feminized by a number of means, the most obvious of which is that he is set up 'as an enigmatic figure, whose demystification and final punishment [...] constitutes [sic] the main narrative goal' (Murray 1993: 293). This is in contra-distinction to the mechanism by which the classic narrative film allegedly operates. According to Mulvey and others, it is the enigma of female sexuality that keeps the masculine viewer riveted to the spectacle. The internal logic of certain generic conventions echoes this relation, particularly the *film noir* which uses the scintillating figure of the *femme fatale* as a fascinating foil to the quest of the hard-boiled detective. In *Monsieur Hire*, however, it is Hire rather than Alice who is constructed as a sexual enigma. Alice's 'secret' (that she is her boyfriend's accomplice) is revealed halfway through the film. Hire's enigma, on the other hand, unsolved and prematurely fore-closed in his death, aligns him with a long tradition of cinematic women rather than men. The association of Hire with women occurs within the diegetic world as well: we are told that he has a criminal record for indecent exposure, which links him with Alice who admits that she takes pleasure in being looked at ('c'est agréable d'être regardée'[16]). Moreover, and very significantly, the police surveillance to which Hire is constantly subjected casts him also as the most obvious victim of the dominant gaze.

Jean Duffy takes this discussion further by proposing that 'the application of the term 'voyeur' to Hire is [...] rendered problematical by the presence within the film of so many other voyeurs' (Duffy 2002: 218). These include the detective (a surveillance 'professional'); Alice herself, who returns M. Hire's gaze, watching him as he watches her make love to her boyfriend (only Émile is the unaware object of the gaze in that scene); and the various women, neighbours and children who suspiciously observe M. Hire's movements. The camera, too, moves between unobtrusive 'naturalistic' shots and self-consciously voyeuristic ones, such as the high camera angle which looks down on Hire's walk to work, tracking him across the courtyard in the manner of a surveillance camera.

What is more, the objects of the gaze are equally numerous. They are: Pierrette's dead body; Alice; Hire; Alice's fiancé Émile, when Hire watches him make love to Alice; as well as numerous inanimate objects of contemplation including dead mice. Several players are both watcher and watched; predator and prey at different moments in the film. The presence of several watchers and several objects of the gaze creates a multi-layered and self-reflexive cinema. Moreover, by pluralizing the dominant-passive object-subject structure of the gaze, Leconte allows the debate to move beyond the limits of the gendered relation described by Mulvey, and into the realm of other ethical debates. Jean Duffy points out that although M. Hire's Jewishness (he is actually M. Hirovitch, of Russian-Armenian descent) is accorded less obvious significance in Leconte's version than in Simenon's novel or Duvivier's *Panique* (1946), it nonetheless functions as a silent subtext which allows Leconte to construct a properly allegorical tale of persecution (Duffy 2002: 219).

It has been argued that Leconte has effectively replaced the signifiers of Jewishness with signifiers of perversion in *Monsieur Hire*, such that the marginality in question is sexual rather than religious/ethnic (Wild 1996). I have pointed out above that it is Hire rather than

16 'it's nice to be watched'

Alice who is the siphon of sexual mystery in the film, skewing the convention of the *femme fatale*. It is certainly true that the nature of Hire's sexuality is put into question several times. One could almost say, indeed, that the 'secret' the spectator searches out with regard to Hire is his *sexual* secret rather than the truth of whether he is Pierrette's murderer (though the two are presumed to be linked, at least by the detective). When the detective goads Hire: 'ça fait combien de temps que vous n'avez pas joui dans une femme?',[17] he evokes the post-sexological, post-Freudian stereotype of the sexually repressed male whose frustration is channelled into violence. The detective assumes that Hire is a lust murderer, while in fact the motive for Pierrette's crime has been robbery. Thus, perverse sexuality is assumed to be the primary underlying motivation in the society evoked in *Monsieur Hire*. If we read the film as a study of the ways in which access to the individual's sexual secret makes him/her into an object of knowledge and societal control, it bears comparison with a Foucauldian analysis of the functioning of knowledge and power. Foucault posits that modernity constructs the sexual secret as the secret *per se* and that it accrues knowledge of the sexuality of its subjects by exhorting them to confess (Foucault 1976). The confession Foucault has in mind is the narrative invited by the sexologist or psychoanalyst and crafted by the analysand, but the role of the policeman functions in *Monsieur Hire* in a similar way: to tease out sexual confession in order to classify the subject (as a deviant criminal).

However, just as the film upsets the assumption of a dominant-submissive logic of the gaze with its pan-voyeuristic perspective, so it sets up not only Hire, but every character, as potentially embodying one or more 'types' of sexual perversion. Thus, the very notion of sexual normalcy recedes from the picture and the meaning of the normal/perverse binarism is similarly put into question by the film's logic. Alice is shown to have exhibitionist tendencies – she enjoys being watched by Hire as she undresses, and becomes erotically aroused when he touches her clandestinely in the very public sphere of the boxing match. Hire is a voyeur, an exhibitionist and fetishist. He frequents prostitutes and is prone to violent outbursts of sexual rage in their presence. He is also a sensualist, who fetishizes scents and textures (he buys a bottle of the perfume Alice uses in order to

17 'how long is it since you came inside a woman?'

evoke her via her scent). The detective displays voyeuristic and sadistic tendencies in his treatment of Hire and a fixation with the (beautifully lit) dead body of Pierrette, which borders on the necrophiliac. Only Émile is the exception to this collection of 'perverts' that would not be out of place in Krafft-Ebing's *Psychopathia Sexualis* (1886).[18] Émile is a murderer for financial rather than sexual gain, and is seen as a representative of the order of heterosexual and masculine normalcy. Alice comments early on in the film, 'j'aime ton façon de m'embrasser. Je trouve que tu m'embrasses comme un homme'.[19] The portrayal of 'ideal' masculinity is, however, subtly ironized and undermined by Leconte: the one 'real man' in the piece is also a brutal murderer and is unwittingly spied upon and cuckolded by the scapegoat M. Hire.

Thus the three main characters (the detective, Hire and Alice) are connected by tacit similarities rather than, as might at first appear likely, radical differences. Any difference in their fates is attributable to the positions they occupy in relation to the social order they find themselves in. Hire is presented as an anti-social misfit. Leconte shows how his status as victim and outsider is constructed according to an arbitrary division between sanctioned and unsanctioned positions and behaviour within the symbolic system of the law. When Alice first catches Hire watching her she tells him that, if she wanted to, she could have him arrested, as there is a law against spying on people. The detective is presented as an equally strange (and much less sympathetic) individual than Hire, but, as an agent of the law, his persecution and surveillance of Hire and gratuitous voyeurism (e.g. of the corpse) go unchallenged. Hire is punishable *only* because he does not have the symbolic means to ensure that he is not. Hire's self-deprecating demeanour and presence suggest that the character recognizes his own disenfranchisement and internalizes the persecution of society.

This subtle critique of the power of the gaze as operating in a more complex and fluid relation than that of an obvious dominant-subordinate couple may remind us of Foucault's discussion of the panopticon in *Surveiller et punir* (1975). The panopticon is an architectural model designed for surveillence: 'à la périphérie un bâtiment

18 An encyclopedic nineteenth-century work of sexology that classified types of sexual deviant by the Austrian-born Richard von Krafft-Ebing.
19 'I like the way you kiss me. I find that you kiss me like a real man'

en anneau; au centre, une tour; celle ci est percée de larges fenêtres qui ouvrent sur la face intérieure de l'anneau'[20] (Foucault 1975: 233). The guard in the middle of the tower can thereby, at any time, watch each of the prisoners in the cells around the inside of the walled building. The effect of this spatial arrangement is to 'induire chez le détenu un état conscient et permanent de visibilité qui assure le fonctionnement automatique du pouvoir'[21] (Foucault 1975: 234). Oppression, then, works by suggestion and by the operation of a (mis)recognition of guilt on the subject's part, rather than by the exercise of force. By analogy then, Hire is constructed by the law as the subject of the legitimate voyeur's gaze. His culpability and punishment are assured not by the hands of individual agents, but by a social organization that rests upon the self-regulating power of surveillance.

The effect of this pluralization of the possession of gaze and perverse desire across the *dramatis personae* of *Monsieur Hire* is twofold. Firstly, it complicates an understanding of watching and desiring as something done by an active (masculine) subject to a passive (feminine) object; and secondly, it draws attention to the ethical groundlessness of the persecution of Hire upon which the film's plot rests. *Monsieur Hire* read in this light is more comparable to a Foucauldian critique of sexual knowledge and surveillance than an account of the gaze and sexuality explicable in Freudian terms. It is my contention, then, that Leconte's film problematizes not only the rules of the gendered gaze, as Murray and Duffy have shown, but also the straightforward conceptual mechanisms we have at our disposal to describe types of desire and relationality that rely on unequal subject–object distribution and the absolute meanings of passivity and activity.

My reading of the film illustrates the dangers of applying wholesale doctrinal feminist film criticism or a model of reading based on the psychoanalytically informed assumption that cinematic representation is always already – and only – about a shared directorial-spectatorial desire. Despite being at first glance an apparently exemplary film with which to test gendered theories of the gaze, as it engages directly with the subject matter of desirous voyeurism, *Monsieur Hire*

20 'around the periphery, a ring-shaped building; in the centre, a tower. The tower has large windows that open out on to the inner facing wall of the ring'
21 'induce in the inmate an awareness of his permanent visibility which ensures the automatic functioning of power'

is much more simultaneously knowing and challenging of the discourses that name subject positions and desires than has previously been recognized. By addressing and problematizing (thematically and structurally) both the gaze and perverse sexuality, the film forces a meta-filmic and meta-theoretical engagement with the silenced ethical implications underpinning gaze theory. Put more simply, by demonstrating the moral innocence of a 'deviant' voyeur, Leconte's film invites a reflection that does not straightforwardly demonize the gaze *or* fall into easy assumptions about the inevitability of the relation between desire and oppression, sexuality and objectification.

## Some concluding remarks

The repeated focus on the theme and stylistics of the gaze in Leconte's films marks a working through of anxieties that are not only personal to the director, but central to the history of the representational arts and inherent to the dynamics of spectatorship which have been theorized by Metz, Mulvey and others as intrinsically voyeuristic and fetishistic.

Two dangers inherent in the use of psychoanalytically informed cinema criticism have been implicitly addressed in the readings in this chapter. Firstly, since the unconscious is by definition unknowable, attributing choice of subject matter/filming technique to unconscious phantasy necessarily delimits the possibility of interpretations allowing for satire, playfulness or parody. Secondly, applying monolithic diagnostic labels of perversion (voyeurism, fetishism, sadism, etc.) to the universal practices of cinema (viewing, filming, composing an image) risks denying the richness of individual and contingent desiring and identifying phantasies and culturally specific meaning-making practices. Effectively, then, cultural and psychical specificity are silenced and difference elided by such models.

It is my contention that, at its richest, the filmic medium can subvert, question or show up the blindspots of the assumptions underpinning film theory. In *Le Parfum d'Yvonne*, the director's complicity with the desire of the heterosexual male protagonist is so strong that despite various devices that work to rupture the fetishistic collusion and question the convention of the male gaze on the female body, it is never successfully decentred. Owing to its subject matter and structure, *Le Mari de la coiffeuse* can be fruitfully put into dialogue with traditions of literary representation and certain psychoanalytic concepts. The film offers retroactive reflection on the preoccupations of the *récit* and the nineteenth-century *conte*/novel. However, in mimicking, rather than simply alluding to, these literary models, the film repeats their logics (the male voicing of the tale, the inevitable death of the woman). Thus, despite some moments of self-questioning, the film is in thrall to the death-driven compulsion it seeks to illustrate. It fetishizes not only Mathilde's body and death, but also the literary and filmic genres it evokes. This reification effectively fixes the film in reactionary codes.

It is precisely in its undoing of fixed categories that *Monsieur Hire* is most successful. It effectively mobilizes meanings where the other films discussed in the chapter conserve them. *Monsieur Hire* treats voyeurism and fetishism thematically and holds them at a sufficient distance to be able to critique the ways in which these mechanisms operate socially and interpersonally. By showing up the differences within constructed categories with regard to power and resistance (legitimized, as distinct from persecuted forms of voyeurism and fetishism), the film moves closer to a deconstructive Foucauldian comment on sexuality and surveillance and avoids reproducing an *unquestioning* version of those mechanisms in filmic form. It thereby poses challenges to methods of film criticism that rely upon theories of the gaze as masculine, patriarchal and universal.

## References

Andrew, Geoff (1990), 'On Voyeurism', *Time Out*, 1027, 25 April–2 May, 37.

Austin, Guy (1996), *Contemporary French Cinema: An Introduction*, Manchester, Manchester University Press.

Baudelaire, Charles (1975), *Œuvres complètes*, vol. 1, Claude Pichois (ed.), Gallimard, Paris.

Bright, Martin (1994), '*Le Parfum d'Yvonne*', *Sight and Sound*, September, 44.

Clover, Carol J. (1992), *Men, Women and Chainsaws*, Princeton, Princeton University Press.

Copperman, Annie (1990), 'Fou d'amour fou', *Les Echos*, 3 October.

Dijkstra, Bram (1986), *Idols of Perversity: Fantasies of Feminine Evil in Fin-de-siècle Culture*, Oxford, Oxford University Press.

Downing, Lisa (2003), *Desiring the Dead: Necrophilia and Nineteenth-Century French Literature*, Oxford, EHRC.

Duffy, Jean H. (2002), 'Message Versus Mystery and Film Noir Borrowings in Patrice Leconte's *Monsieur Hire*', *French Cultural Studies*, 13: 2, 38, 209–24.

Flaubert, Gustave ([1857] 1972), *Madame Bovary*, Paris, Gallimard.

Foucault, Michel (1975), *Surveiller et punir: Naissance de la prison*, Paris, Gallimard.

Foucault, Michel (1976) *Histoire de la sexualité 1: La volonté de savoir*, Paris, Gallimard.

Freud, Sigmund ([1915/1916] 1988), 'On Transcience', Pelican Freud Library 14 *Art and Literature: Jensen's 'Gradiva', Leonardo da Vinci and Other Works*, Harmondsworth, Penguin, 287–90.

Freud, Sigmund ([1920] 1991), *Beyond the Pleasure Principle*, Penguin Freud Library 11 *On Metapsychology*, Harmondsworth, Penguin, 269–338.

Freud, Sigmund ([1927] 1991), 'Fetishism', Penguin Freud Library 7 *On Sexuality*, Harmondsworth, Penguin, 344–57.

Handyside, Fiona (2003), 'Possessing Stars, Possessing Texts: Jeanne Moreau and the New Wave', in Julia Horn and Lindsey Russell-Watts (eds), *Possessions: Essays in French Literature, Cinema and Theory*, Bern, Peter Lang, 55–66.

Haskell, Molly (1997), *Holding My Own in No Man's Land: Women and Men and Feminism and Film*, Oxford, Oxford University Press.

Leconte, Patrice (2000), *Je suis un imposteur*, Paris, Flammarion.

Lemire, Elise (2000), 'Voyeurism and the Post-war Crisis of Masculinity in *Rear Window*', in John Belton (ed.), *Alfred Hitchcock's Rear Window*, Cambridge, Cambridge University Press, 57–90.

Metz, Christian ([1975] 1985), 'Story/discourse: Notes on Two Kinds of Voyeurism', in Bill Nichols (ed.), *Movies and Methods*, vol. 2, London, Berkeley, Los Angeles, University of California Press, 543–9.

Mulvey, Laura (1975), 'Visual Pleasure and Narrative Cinema', *Screen*, 16: 3, autumn, 6–18.

Mulvey, Laura (1981), 'Afterthoughts on "Visual Pleasure and Narrative Cinema" inspired by King Vidor's *Duel in the Sun* (1946)', *Framework*, 15/16/17, 12–15.

Murphy, Kathleen (1992), 'La Belle Dame sans merci', *Film Comment*, 28: 6, 28–30.

Murray, Abigail (1993), 'Voyeurism in *Monsieur Hire*', *Modern and Contemporary France*, 3, July, 287–95.

Rose, Louise (1988) 'Freud and Fetishism: Previously Unpublished Minutes of the Vienna Psychoanalytic Society', *Psychoanalytic Quarterly*, 57: 2, 147–65.

Segal, Naomi (1988), *Narcissus and Echo: Women in the French Récit*, Manchester, Manchester University Press.

Studlar, Gaylin (1988), *In the Realm of Pleasure: Von Sternberg, Dietrich and the Masochistic Aesthetic*, Urbana, University of Illinois.

Sutton, Paul (1999), '*Afterwardsness* in Film: Patrice Leconte's *Le Mari de la coiffeuse*', *French Studies*, 53: 3, July, 307–17.

Wild, Floriane (1996), 'L'Histoire ressuscitée: Jewishness and Scapegoating in Julien Duvivier's *Panique*', in Steven Ungar and Tom Conley (eds), *Identity Papers: Contested Nationhood in Twentieth-Century France*, Minneapolis, University of Minnesota Press, 178–92.

# 5

# The ethics of the couple

> The pathos of love consists in the insurmountable duality of beings. Love is a relationship with that which is forever concealed. This relationship does not neutralize the alterity, but conserves it. The pathos of desire rests in the fact of being two. The other as other is not an object bound to become mine or become me; it retreats on the contrary into its mystery. (Emmanuel Levinas)

In recent years (1999–2002), Leconte has made a series of films which suggest an obsession with the subject matter of *l'amour fou* (mad love), leading to self-sacrifice, transcendence or death. *La Fille sur le pont*, *La Veuve de Saint-Pierre*, *Félix et Lola* and *Rue des plaisirs*, made consecutively and within the space of three years, all take unconventional love as their thematic pivot; even if each film recasts love in different generic and aesthetic colours. Indeed, in a recent interview, Leconte states: 'J'ai l'impression en ce moment que le cinéma est fait pour raconter des histoires d'amour'[1] (Thirard and Tobin 2002: 32). This trend was only broken – or at least modified – in 2003 with *L'Homme du train*, which renounced the focus on the heterosexual couple in favour of a return to the male friendship model. However, regardless of the shift in the sex of the protagonists, the emotional depth of the representation and certain shared motifs (chance, responsibility, difference, death) make this film very much a part of the series in question. Despite the unashamed romanticism that pervades certain of these films and touches, at moments, on a rather excessive sentimentality (most obviously seen in *Rue des plaisirs*, the weakest of the series), Leconte's treatment of love is not,

1 'At the moment I have the feeling that cinema was made for telling love stories'

for the most part, devoid of a deeper ethical content. On the contrary, in focusing on the romantic couple, or revisiting the devoted pair of the male friendship model in *L'Homme du train*, Leconte insists upon the demands of responsibility, sacrifice and self-questioning attendant upon intersubjectivity. In so doing, he echoes one of the key concerns that preoccupies contemporary French thought: the quest for a viable ethics in late modernity or postmodernity. Ethical debates in the Continental school have shifted away from a practical focus on rights, duty and social equality to a consideration of the more abstract question of how to respect the incommensurability of the other. Thus, the broader, socio-political dimension of ethics has been downplayed in favour of investigations of more intimate configurations of inter-relatedness.

In Thirard and Tobin's interview with Leconte, the director comments, 'Je ne m'excuse pas. Je ne suis pas un cinéaste témoin de son temps "engagé" [...] je préfère l'imagination à un état des lieux de la société française ou mondiale'[2] (Thirard and Tobin 2002: 30). This reluctance to comment on the social specificities of a given epoch echoes numerous similar statements made elsewhere by the director, and discussed in other contexts in the present book. His dogged insistence on the imperative to 's'abstraire de toute datation possible' and to concentrate upon the 'côté intemporel'[3] of a given *mise en scène* (even in historical films such as *Ridicule* or *La Veuve de Saint-Pierre*) means that his concerns as a filmmaker are abstracted from the level of historical or cultural specificity and attain the level of the philosophical.

When Leconte identifies love as the most appropriate subject matter for contemporary cinema and foregrounds the 'moral party of two'[4] as a privileged site of exploration of human capacities, he echoes the preoccupations of the philosophy of Emmanuel Levinas. Put simply, Levinas, like Leconte, locates the ethical in the dimension of the spontaneous encounter with the other, which calls the subject to a consciousness of his or her own responsibility. Erotic love, for Levinas,

---

2 'I make no apology for it. I am not a committed filmmaker concerned with bearing witness to the Zeitgeist [...] I privilege imagination over commentary on contemporary French or global society.'

3 'avoid as far as possible period detail'; 'atemporal aspect'

4 The phrase is taken from the title of a chapter of Zygmunt Bauman's *Postmodern Ethics* (1993).

serves as a fundamental metaphor for the ethical relation, in which the subject 'caresses' rather than 'possesses' the other in a dynamic of infinite respect (Levinas [1961] 1969: 256–66). I argued in chapter 3 that demonstrating the dynamics of the masculine masquerade affords Leconte an opportunity for thinking and filming a *rapprochement* between the sexes by stressing the common exigency to perform and dissimulate identities. Thus, what appears initially as an exclusion of female subjectivity can be read against the grain as an attempt to approach it. Similarly, the turn away from the political towards the imaginary realm of the interpersonal encounter signals not a retreat from ethical concerns but – paradoxically – a return to them.

It is my contention, then, that in these recent works, Leconte exploits the filmic language of love as a metaphor for broader ethical challenges, encounters and dilemmas in ways that parallel the contexts in which Levinas's work is starting to be considered within recent theoretical debates. For Zygmunt Bauman, Levinas has become the exemplary ethical thinker of postmodernism by posing 'an ethics that readmits the Other as a neighbour [...] that restores the autonomous moral significance of proximity' (Bauman 1993: 84). For Marc-Alain Ouaknin, Levinas is postmodern because he proposes 'the strategy of opening, which breaks the monadic immanence and makes the subject into one-that-steps-outside-of-itself, the subject of self-transcendence' (cited in Bauman 1993: 84–5).

Leconte's recent films, especially *La Fille sur le pont* and *La Veuve de Saint-Pierre*, offer mature reworkings of the dynamics of identity and relatedness presented in, for example, *Le Mari de la coiffeuse*. The maturation in question involves a more sophisticated distancing from the ideologies underpinning mythic constructions of identity that are merely parodied in earlier films. This occurs in tandem with, and via, a pursuit of the postmodern technique of pastiche. Pastiche destabilizes, rather than merely shows up, the workings of latent ideologies by refusing to reference the context and 'original' meaning of given conventions. It effects an emptying out of the associations of the modern tradition and opens up models of relatedness for renovation of meaning. Leconte's heterosexual love stories offer portrayals of unconventional couples that, at their best moments, fragment existing conventions of representation. This is visible particularly in the portrayal of femininity. The women portrayed in these films are complex characters whose motivations and personal histories are three-dimensional and yet elude total comprehension or assimilation. This means that neither the director, nor the viewer, nor the male protagonist, may possess the female figure. Rather than being reduced and interpreted by strategies of fetishism or decoding by the male, she floats free; integral in her alterity. For Levinas, the careful maintenance of the irreducibility of the other is at the heart of ethics: 'the very value of love is the impossibility of reducing the Other to myself, to co-inciding into sameness' (Levinas cited in Cohen 1986: 22). Thus, despite the commonplace which holds that postmodern aesthetic modes are consonant with an ethical deadness, I shall be asserting in this chapter that the postmodern composition of Leconte's later films is indistinguishable from a contemporary ethical agenda.

One could perhaps object to my ethical reading of Leconte's films by pointing out that he portrays ethical encounters with otherness in the context only of the white, heterosexual subject. Encounters between sexually, racially or ethnically diverse others could add depth and the necessary acknowledgement of cultural and subjective relativism to Leconte's ethical portrayals. While this is for the most part true, I will go on to demonstrate that he deconstructs the meaning of heterosexuality in *La Fille sur le pont* and implicitly addresses the condition of the colonized (French Canadian) other in *La Veuve de Saint-Pierre*. Moreover – and crucially – the heterosexual couple in love may be read not as an unquestioned norm or the assumption of a universal on the director's part, but as a reference to a long-standing cinematic convention, a template adopted in the interests of denaturalizing the ideologies subtending its construction.

## From obscure objects of desire to irreducible others

It is possible to argue that throughout Leconte's production, there is an attempt to allow his female protagonists to remain unknowable and therefore to preserve their status as wholly other. One could posit, for example, that the apparent one-dimensionality of Mathilde the hairdresser in *Le Mari de la coiffeuse*, the refusal of any exploration of her motivation, actually bespeaks a desire to leave her experience intact, individuated. However, as I have shown in the previous chapter, the conventionality of the *récit* form which structures Mathilde's tale forces the viewer to understand her identity by reference to literary traditions and clichés. In the films under discussion in this chapter, Leconte avoids this impasse somewhat by shattering the unity of the formal aesthetic and the thematic premises of the love story, in such a way as to avoid inevitable recourse to the meanings of pre-existing codes and conventions.

*La Fille sur le pont* works on many levels to construct an antidote to *Le Mari de la coiffeuse*. The implied allusion I noted in *Le Mari de la coiffeuse* to the heroine who jumps in Truffaut's New Wave classic *Jules et Jim* (1962) is picked up again here and its meaning subtly subverted. Where *Le Mari de la coiffeuse* reaches narrative closure with Mathilde's suicidal jump from the bridge, the action of *La Fille sur le pont* is *triggered* by Adèle's leap. Paradis's character becomes the new-millennial version of the cinematic heroine: she is Catherine/Mathilde modernized and mobilized. The woman's suicidal gesture functions as a springboard to narrative mobility and provokes Gabor (Auteuil) to ethical action, rather than serving as a naturalized conclusion.

This is not the only New Wave allusion in the film. The aesthetic of *La Fille sur le pont* is stylistically reminiscent of the *cinéma des auteurs*, with its use of black and white *cinéma-vérité* camerawork. Ginette Vincendeau has pointed out that the opening scene of the film, which shows Adèle being interviewed and invited to recount her life story, echoes Truffaut's depiction of Antoine Doinel's interview with a psychologist in *Les Quatre cents coups* (1959) (Vincendeau, 2000: 44). While this allusion is no doubt part of Leconte's intertextual artillery here, I would argue that the figure of Adèle is in fact more reminiscent of Godard's cinema than Truffaut's, and particularly that it echoes *A bout de souffle* (1959). Adèle is transformed within the narrative by means of a haircut from a long-haired urchin to a chic page boy, a style that resembles Jean Seberg's token blonde crop in that film. And, while Mathilde was associated with the hairdresser's salon which she seldom left (except to kill herself), Adèle becomes a road movie heroine, a mobile *flâneuse*, in the manner of Seberg's character in Godard's film, who walks in the street and does not die at the end of the film. Thus, Adèle abandons the classic feminine appearance and behaviour of Mathilde for the ultra-modern, andro-gynous haircut and lifestyle of a postmodern Seberg. Moreover, her transformation is wrought *as we watch*, suggesting a demystification of the processes of feminine performativity rather than the natural-istic construction of female beauty we associate with the glamour of cinema. The scenes from *La Fille sur le pont* in which Gabor restyles Adèle are reminiscent of the sequence in Luc Besson's postmodern thriller, *Nikita* (1990), in which an aged and resplendent Jeanne Moreau shows the young female assassin how to make up her face and do her hair. Thus, what is usually an essential part of cinema's mystique is placed on the surface of the spectacle and made transparent *as performance*.

In tandem with this presentation of a heroine that is self-deconstructive with regard to the performances of femininity, the cinematic treatment of the woman's body differs considerably in *Le Mari de la coiffeuse* and *La Fille sur le pont*. Where Mathilde's body was subject to multiple close-ups, with particular attention brought to her breasts as fetishistic talismans of the maternal body of Schaeffer, Adèle is shot in such a way as to emphasize the ludicity and pastiche of the presentation, and a certain self-awareness regarding the conventions of framing the female. Most of the frames that focus on Paradis's body take place during scenes of knife-throwing. I explored in chapter 3 the ways in which the workings of the masculine masquerade were exposed by focusing on characters who are performers within the diegetic world, such as Rochefort's Mortez in *Tandem*, or the 'grands ducs'. By making Gabor and Adèle circus performers – a type of performance, moreover, that requires particularly exaggerated gesture, appearance and feats of danger – Leconte again foregrounds the performativity of identities. This means that when he films Paradis's body as a spectacle, it is within a context in which it is already set up as a target, not only for the gaze but for Gabor's flying knives.

The knife-throwing display suggests three associated ideas: the gaze, sexual penetration and erotic domination. Certain critics refuse to read the motif as ludic, and instead see it as a symptom of Leconte's alleged misogyny. Ginette Vincendeau, for example, is troubled by the implicit violence in the knife-throwing metaphor which, she argues, 'turns both farcical and nasty, as Paradis passively waits to be wounded' (Vincendeau 2000: 44). Indeed, the potential danger of the act is an important level of signification. The masculine cinematic gaze that *figuratively* annihilates the woman by objectifying her is literalized by Leconte as the flight of the knife that risks her *bodily* death. However, the bodily 'risk' in knife-throwing is habitually silenced by the presence of play at work in the spectacle: a circus audience enjoys the thrill of danger to the target, while recuperating their sadism as harmless pleasure in seeing a show. The seduction of the cinematic spectacle works in the same way, occluding ideology by focusing on the mask of glamour. Similarly, when Adèle is shown erotically enjoying the knife-throwing, we might think of the pleasure of being looked at that is a politically questionable, but nonetheless predominant, response to the objectifying gaze. Leconte's motifs thus highlight the ways in which these problematic meanings are both articulated and disavowed in the traditional cinematic – or circus – spectacle.

As far as the sexual dimension of the knife-throwing goes, one cannot avoid the observation that the link between sexual penetration and the gaze is a commonplace of post-Lacanian psychoanalytic theory. The gaze (as the desirous, intensified look which overcomes the fear of castration) is a phantasy mechanism, just as the phallus is a phantasy of masculine potency. To substitute knives for the phallus is to demonstrate the imaginary sadism of the phallic economy, all the while pointing to the gap between illusion and reality. I have already argued elsewhere that to read the knife-throwing motif in this film as either erotically titillating or downright misogynistic is to misread as 'straight' Leconte's presentation (Downing 2002). Instead, the deliberate theatricality of the scenes with the knives, intensified by the self-consciously hyperbolic musical score that accompanies them, works to demystify rather than shore up the myth that the penis can ever be the phallus. Leconte's knife-throwing is thus an overdetermined parodic spectacle which mocks simultaneously the phallic ambitions of the penis in heteronormativity, and the myth that transcendental truth may lie in the processes of symbolization. Rather than reinforcing these masculine myths, the motif may instead remind us of the immanence of simulacra (see Downing 2002: 37).

Knife-throwing, in the context of this film that quotes from and recycles cinematic conventions of feminine construction in a post-modern mode, becomes an apt visual metaphor for the convention of cinematic representation, whereby the director 'shoots' and 'cuts' the image of the other. The exhilarating celebration of filming/knife-throwing is seen in Leconte's work alongside a paradoxical conscious-ness of their morally dubious or violent dimension. Leconte's own cinema is inevitably implicated in this process – it cannot transcend its own form – but it does not simply or uncritically reproduce it.

Instead, it shows up its mechanisms, sounding an ethical warning alongside the cinematic celebration of visual excess and aesthetic pleasure.

This is not the only example one could take from Leconte's late films of a self-conscious literalization of the tacit erotic violence of the conventions of heterosexuality/representation for the purposes of undermining those meanings. In *Rue des plaisirs*, a piece of dialogue between the lovers, Dimitri (Vincent Elbaz) and Marion (Lætitia Casta), is similarly suggestive. In a dreamy love scene that takes place in a stationary train carriage, Dimitri tells Marion that, had he not met her, he would have become a murderer, cutting up a series of women in order to combine their body parts in the quest for a composite perfect woman that would resemble her. This piece of black humour in the service of verbal seduction recalls the cutting up of the female body in close-up shots and editing processes. The language of romantic love ('I love you to pieces!') and the language of cinema coincide in their logic that to love the other is, on some level, to kill the other. Leconte thus forces recognition of the truth of the deceptive violence of idealization, as well as providing an ethical alternative to it. In *Rue des plaisirs*, the self-abasing and altruistic figure of le Petit Louis (Patrick Timsit) embodies a self-sacrificial alternative to Vincent's, however seductive, model of erotic altericide.[5] In *La Fille sur le pont*, the appeal to ethics is more subtle, as the viewer is called upon to recognize the journey undertaken by Gabor and Adèle, a journey to overcome the impulse to instrumentalize the other, and to replace it with a genuinely ethical relation of respect, by means which I shall discuss later in this chapter.

In *La Veuve de Saint-Pierre* and, especially, *Félix et Lola*, an alternative strategy is employed to treat the 'problem' of filming the female in a way that avoids unethical reduction. These films scrupulously avoid a fixing or fragmenting focus on the bodies of 'Madame La' (Binoche) and Lola (Gainsbourg) and instead allow the woman to mobilize the narrative action and create meaning. *Félix et Lola* incorporates many thematic and structural elements of a *polar*: uncertain

---

5 The term 'altericide' (from the Latin 'other' + 'to kill') is used in Levinasian theory (see especially Davis 2000: 12–30). It suggests not (only) literal murder but the violence that the subject does to the other when he or she reduces the other to the same, rather than respecting the ethical challenge of leaving wholly intact the other's difference.

identities, gun toting and a murder that opens the film. However, the refusal to film Gainsbourg's body as an object for pleasurable contemplation and cinematic fetishism is paralleled at the diegetic level by Félix's refusal to engage in the *film noir* game of decoding the woman-enigma. Lola is apparently set up as a figure of mystery: a sad-eyed loner with a secret past. Yet, despite the 'clues' that fall in Félix's path, he maintains his respectful distance: 'Je ne pose pas de questions',[6] and is shown experiencing a conflict between the wish to follow and protect Lola when she disappears for a mysterious and apparently dangerous rendezvous, and his promise to her: 'j'ai confiance en toi, Lola'.[7] He declares a desire to help her without feeling the need to know her life story. The sexual politics set up in the film thus demonstrate a Levinasian ethical dilemma, in which 'Love is the incessant watching over the other' (Levinas cited in Cohen 1986: 30). Rather than spying on her, the incessant watching over of respectful love is revealed as a relinquishing of possessiveness and the desire to control the other.

By setting this postmodern *polar* in a fairground – site of illusion, play and trickery – Leconte undermines the totemic menace of the myth of female mystery that is reified by the *noir* genre. He suggests that just as the feminine masquerade is an illusion, so the male obsession with unmasking is an overdetermined and unethical response to it. The notion of the female masquerade is also dislocated in this film from a tacit and defensive mechanism whereby passive appearance masks symbolic aggression (Rivière's bluestockings replacing assertive speech with a reassuringly harmless appearance) to the level of the verbal. Lola's version of the *femme fatale* is a compulsive liar, a middle-class girl who creates for herself an alternative life story, a more intriguing persona. She is not the *femme fatale* by dint of her disadvantageous positioning vis-à-vis the symbolic order, but by design. She lies in order to propel her own story, create action and manipulate the other. Her actions are unethical, but they allow for a de-hystericization of the masquerade in such a way as to demystify the *noir* convention. Moreover, far from the perfidy of the *femme fatale* leading to the male hero's mortal danger, her lies are relatively harmless ones, operating at the surface of a play of

6 'I won't ask you any questions'
7 'I trust you, Lola'

discourses about identity that take place in the ludic setting of a fairground. Indeed, the whole concept of identity in the film, rather than bearing the weight of a truth effect, is revealed as a series of performative gestures that shatter rather than shore up the myths of ontology.

In parallel, then, with their blank glance rather than desirous gaze on female beauty, these films complicate the notion of decoding or understanding female motivation as the film's 'problem'. Moreover, they do not provide didactic 'morals' or 'meanings'. It is possible to argue that both Félix and the Captain are betrayed by their female lovers' deceptions (Lola's fabrications/Madame La's love for another). However, in both cases, the narrative point of view does not allow for the simplistic reading of female perfidy, and sufficient identification is permitted with both male and female figures to allow a more nuanced and ambiguous ethics to surface. Thus, once the convention of fetishism of the female is removed from the cinematic equation – either by irony or naturalization – the filming of the couple dynamic can move on to a level of equality and difference.

In these progressive and experimental films, then, the woman's body is portrayed in a range of ways that defy the conventional language of appropriation, either by suggesting irony and an ethical appeal to humour that disrupts awe (denaturalization), or by a refusal to frame the female in any of the ways that connote desire (what we might term a 'renaturalization' of the object that has been perpetually the exaggerated focus of the gaze). My contention that this is properly a cinema of equality between the sexes is highlighted also by the director's manipulation of narrative point of view in the four films. Rather than belonging to the male narrator (as in *Le Mari de la coiffeuse* or *Le Parfum d'Yvonne*) the centre of onscreen consciousness is now shared, pluralized and at times ambiguous and impossible to attribute.

Gabor and Adèle in *La Fille sur le pont* share the cinematic point of view more or less equally throughout, in a structural gesture that corroborates the theme of their mutual interdependency (signalled by the motif of the incredible luck they share while together, which deserts them whenever they are separated). Moreover, the opening words of the film are given to Paradis, in her interview with the off-stage female presence, who at first appears to be a psychiatrist, but is later revealed as a television chat show hostess. The staging of the analytic confession on television rather than in a consulting room suggests both the fascination with spectacle and voyeurism that is a precondition of postmodernity, but also the democratization of discourses of identity. When describing her first sexual encounter, Adèle says that it was uncomfortable. The older woman immediately cuts in with the observation that of course, when you are so young, sex is a difficult matter. Without missing a beat, Adèle counters that it was uncomfortable only because it took place in the restroom of a motorway service station and 'c'est pas très pratique'.[8] Thus, Adèle refuses the mental health professional's interpretations of her behaviour and constructs her own story by means of a humour that deconstructs the logic of the do-gooder.

In *La Veuve de Saint-Pierre*, the narrative outcome (the Captain's death) means that Madame La's perception is foregrounded and has the status of narrative authority throughout the film. The fact that it opens with a long shot of Madame La, in widow's garb, gazing out of the window, indicates that the narrative is being recounted at a temporal moment after her husband's death. Her voice-over, which frames the narrative events, confirms that the viewer's identification is thus with Binoche's character from the outset. In *Rue des plaisirs*, the events are narrated by three prostitutes, according the story of the love triangle a pluralized, feminine voicing. In *Félix et Lola*, meanwhile, the point of view is shared between the couple, but incorporates uncertainty, as the film opens and is intercut with flashbacks to an event that never took place (the shooting of Lola's ex-lover by Félix). It is never made clear to whose imagination this event belongs, or if it is the product of an intersubjective fantasy space. By sharing the weight of narrative meaning between the characters, or attributing it to the female rather than the male protagonist, Leconte overcomes the tradition of the *récit* that has been criticized for reducing the female role to spectacle rather than subjectivity.

## Faces of love and death

Despite their many unconventional aspects, these films paradoxically include elements of the traditional romantic narrative, including recourse to discourses of fate and chance, the focus upon doomed

---

8 'it wasn't very practical'

love, and the figure of the *Liebestod* (love-in-death). The blending of elements of the traditional language of love with original or surprising events, outcomes and cinematographic devices confounds straightforward interpretation or linear readings. The figure of death is one of the most challenging of these elements.

Death is a key figure of postmodern ethics. For Slavoj Žižek, the pursuit of the Real of desire involves, in Hegel's terms, an inevitable tarrying with the negative. In the preface of *Phenomenology of Spirit*, Hegel writes: '[T]he life of the Spirit is not the life that shrinks from death and keeps itself untouched by devastation [...] It wins its truth only when, in utter dismemberment, it finds itself' (Žižek 1993, epigraph). The Hegelian model suggests, then, that the truth of Being is paradoxically found precisely there where it most risks annihilation. Žižek's own ethical paradigm involves risking the subject's anchor in the symbolic order, thematized as adherence to politically correct liberal doctrine, in favour of proximity to the truth of desire. In *The Ticklish Subject*, Žižek cites as a contemporary ethical heroine the schoolteacher Mary Kay Letourneau, who sacrificed her professional position for the erotic love of her 14-year-old male pupil. By eschewing symbolic authority for the pursuit of desire in the Real, her professional suicide constituted an authentic ethical act. By 'authentic', Žižek means here a wholly appropriate response to the dominant ideologies of the contemporary moment, in that it demonstrated the self-sameness of moral majority fundamentalists and the liberal left, who reacted with equal outrage couched in similar terms (Žižek 2000: 381–2). Žižek's example demonstrates the broader political significance of acts in the apparently personal sphere and the radical disruptive potential of the erotic couple.

For ethical models based on a Levinasian paradigm, the 'moral party of two' similarly involves an openness to the possibility of self loss: 'The passion of ethics [...], like that of love, comes of movement and questioning. The Other affects the subject, draws it beyond the confines of self and experience and in that movement without return leaves the security of the self and its supporting systems in question' (Botting and Wilson 2002: 93). Žižek and Levinas, then, both describe a rejection of bourgeois models of individual and couple identity in favour of a radical quest (for desire, in Žižek's case, and love in Levinas's), which leaves the subject open to the threat of symbolic death.

Leconte's films similarly eschew bourgeois versions of coupledom in favour of an ethical model of love that incorporates the risk of radical self-dispossession. According to Levinas, the couple in love should not connote a dialectical unity, a closed and insular totality. Rather, the presence of ethics in love allows the dynamic of romantic coupledom to transcend the closed dyad of totality. For Leconte, too, in these films, the couple allows for an opening on to a perception of the infinite, through the figure of death which serves to mobilize the meaning of devotion.

*La Veuve de Saint-Pierre* offers itself as a particularly rich text with which to explore this point. Of the films in question, it is the one with the most obviously 'ethical' thematic concerns, in the conventional as well as the postmodern senses of the term. A consideration of the death penalty debate is juxtaposed with a dilemma of intersubjective respect, centred on the love triangle. While the film was generally well received by critics, one reviewer commented that: 'the politics of *La Veuve de Saint-Pierre* [...] can be reduced to bland slogans along the lines of "Abolish capital punishment" and "beware the wrath of petit-bourgeois functionaries scorned"' (Witt 2000: 57). As the reader will no doubt expect by now, my response to this criticism is the observation that Leconte's treatment of the political sphere is always less sharply observed than the world of the intersubjective encounter or the politics of the imaginary. Indeed, this was an unusual vehicle for Leconte, both in its historical setting and in treating directly a straightforward social issue, and it is not surprising to learn that the film was not originally Leconte's project. He stepped in, citing as his incentives the irresistible lure of working with Binoche and Auteuil (Thirard and Tobin 2002: 30), only when Alain Corneau abandoned it four months prior to the commencement of shooting. I would tend to agree with Witt that the inclusion of this film in the Lecontian *œuvre* probably owes much to the fact that he 'perceived here the opportunity for a further variation on the fine portraits of sexual desire' (Witt 2000: 57) that characterize his earlier work.

This said, the two ethical modes, which we might designate modern and postmodern, coexist in the narrative, such that the dialectic between the 'serious' political (public) sphere and the 'trivial' domestic (private) sphere is effectively overcome. *La Veuve de Saint-Pierre* is structured around a whole nexus of sites of otherness, principally the colonial space, female subjectivity and criminality. The film relays in parallel the sort of ethical challenge I have designated postmodern, and a more traditional dilemma from the realm of moral philosophy. The Captain sacrifices himself apparently for a moral principle (his opposition to the death penalty), but it is just as much a gesture of self-abandonment born of love for his wife and of respect for the murderer, Neel. The action can be understood, then, in relation to an ethics based on a consciousness of interpersonal responsibility rather than social duty.

Levinas describes the encounter with the other via a metaphor of vision. The other appears to the one in the form of 'the face', a spectacle which calls the subject to a consciousness of the vulnerability of alterity and the exigency of respect. It is in this way that, within a Levinasian model, ethics can be said to precede ontology. Moreover, the encounter with the face involves a choice between risk to the self and violence to the other. Levinas writes: 'The epiphany of the face brings forth the possibility of gauging the infinity of the temptation to murder' (Levinas [1961] 1969: 199). *La Veuve de Saint-Pierre* can be read as operating around the repetition of a key structural ethical event: an encounter with the face of the other that provokes either the violence of murder or infinite respect.

The film's exposition includes a flashback to Neel's crime: the apparently motiveless stabbing, while in a drunken state, of an old man, along with his friend Louis Ollivier. The drinking partners' conversation prior to the crime concerns an argument over whether the old man is 'gros' (big) or 'gras' (fat). When asked by the court official why they killed and cut up the victim, Ollivier responds with the absurd logic that it was to establish whether he really was big or fat. Their failed attempt to characterize, interpret and thereby possess the meaning of the other is offered as the causal catalyst to the act of violence. This echoes the idea of the failure of respect for the irreducibility of alterity, and thematizes Levinas's contention that the other's unknowable difference provokes a temptation to annihilate that difference in the act of murder. For Levinas, murder of the other (a single human being) is the banal act through which the one attempts to annihilate the Other, that is to obliterate the frightening trace of difference that bears witness to the incommensurability of beings external to oneself (Levinas [1961] 1969: 198).

The second encounter posed in the film is between the law and Neel. His enigmatic crime, with its apparent lack of understandable motive, similarly calls forth a temptation to punishing retribution. In the death penalty, what Levinas would call the 'infinite temptation to murder' appears in a form that is culturally codified and sanctioned. However, the narrative incorporates a twist as Saint-Pierre does not possess a guillotine or an executioner, and the tortuous process traversed by the authorities in order to procure both suggests a loss of innocence and the forced interiorization by the colonized community of an other law.

The meeting of the political and the personal, and the collapsing of their arbitrary boundaries that the film works to achieve, are crystallized in a key *double entendre*: the 'veuve' of the title. 'Veuve' means 'widow' and is also a slang term for 'guillotine'. The encounter between the colonial site of Paris and the subordinate Canadian island is metaphorically thematized by the repeated occurrence of the ominous image of the boat crossing the sea and bringing the instrument of death to Saint-Pierre. Equally, however, 'veuve' suggests Binoche's character, the widow of the title, introduced in the opening frames in her mourning garb. Thus, she is positioned as inhabited by loss even before we are allowed to understand how her loss came about. Moreover, the temporal and ideological division signalled by the difference between Paris and Saint-Pierre – one of premodernity and modernity – is located also on the site of femininity, embodied here by the widow, Madame La. The Captain's respect for La's ethical project of rehabilitating Neel leads to his being ridiculed by fellow officers, in a social milieu and historical moment in which women have lower civic status than men and no political voice.

Finally, the encounter between the Captain and Madame La and the murderer Neel allows for a further set of ethical reflections. The married couple is portrayed in numerous scenes as very obviously engaged in a passionate sexual relationship. Establishing their devotion for each other allows an element of unfathomability to enter into the picture: why would Madame La encourage the sacrifice of such a devoted husband to try to save a convicted killer? The illogic of this ethics of coupledom, its capacity to go beyond itself and outstrip an understanding of reason, marks out Leconte's portrayal as belonging to the same postmodern strand as Ouaknin identifies with regard to Levinas. The subject in love in *La Veuve de Saint-Pierre* is properly 'one-that-steps-outside-of-itself, the subject of self-transcendence' (cited in Bauman 1993: 84–5).

The rules that are accorded importance in socially sanctioned relationships (epitomized by emotional and sexual fidelity in marriage) are superseded in the film's logic by a more transcendental code of fidelity. The Captain's love for his wife is not undermined or compromised by her love for Neel; he does not feel betrayed, humiliated or slighted by it. The only mention of sexual jealousy between the couple in the film comes, significantly, in the form of a joke: Madame La playfully declares herself jealous of her husband's affection for his beloved horse. Their relationship of absolute trust is presented as a counter-discourse to the gossip and petty speculation of the Captain's colleagues and to bourgeois mores. The presence of Neel does not compromise the union of the two, rather it creates a third ethical space into which the configuration of ethical love presented by the Captain and his wife can extend. As Levinas would have it: 'Love [...] can never be satisfied or contented with the bourgeois ideal of love as domestic comfort or as the mutual possession of two people living out an *egoisme-à-deux*' (Levinas cited in Cohen 1986: 30).

The film closes with a scene in which the different ethical spheres to which the narrative alludes are collapsed on to each other. The Captain's execution is portrayed via a cinematographically stunning frame of Auteuil, whose white shirt is stained with vivid blood, teetering on the brink of death against a background of shimmering blue sea. The *tricolore* created in this image adumbrates the symbol of the French nation to which the Captain belongs and whose Colonial power has brought him as a stranger to the island. The ethereal image of the nation – projected on to the body of a dying man and against the backdrop of a waterway rather than a land mass, a *terre patrie* – suggests an awareness of the historically contingent meanings of the nation state.[9] The death of the Captain, then, is called upon to suggest the fluid nature of fixed gendered/national narratives in moments of cultural-historical instability, both in the period evoked within the diegesis (premodernity/modernity) and in the contemporary moment (late modernity/post-modernity). Death in this final frame is thus figured as movement and flux, and the captain's self-sacrificial act as a transcendental bridge between modes of being belonging to the past, present and future.

9 This idea was inspired by Bill Marshall's as yet unpublished work on the concept of the 'French Atlantic'. See his forthcoming introduction, 'The French Atlantic', in *Encyclopaedia of French-American Relations*, ed. Bill Marshall (forthcoming).

One of the other ways in which Leconte foregrounds death as inherent to the ethics of love is by means of an eroticization and idealization of it. This is a problematic gesture, as it can at first sight seem to echo conservatively the long artistic tradition of death-driven eroticism, as analysed in my discussion of *Le Mari de la coiffeuse*, which is often tainted with misogynist gender politics and a dynamic of appropriation and objectification. However, I would argue that the foregrounding of erotic death here is in the interests of renovation rather than reactionary repetition. This is a death-driven eroticism that is paradoxically made mobile: not so much perversion or paraphilia as parody or play.

This point is best illustrated with reference to *La Fille sur le pont*. The film establishes proximity between scenes of promiscuous sexual intercourse (Adèle has sex with numerous young men she meets on her travels including a train passenger, a contortionist and a waiter) and scenes of knife-throwing with Gabor. While most of the knife-throwing scenes take place on stage, as a public display, in one memorable case the ritual is reenacted in private for the pleasure of the participants. In the sequence in question, we cut from a scene of Adèle in the arms of an amorous Italian waiter to a scene in which she seeks out Gabor to request a sexual service ('tu sais de quoi j'ai envie?'). This question of 'what the woman wants' in the sphere of the sexual is answered here with some irony: she wants to have knives thrown at her. The dynamic at work in the knife-throwing – one of apparent sado-masochistic erotic interaction – is used by Leconte to highlight the difficulty of interpreting the power relations underpinning *all* erotic exchange. In the scene in which the two engage in knife-throwing behind the railway lines, Leconte films the activity in such a way as to suggest Adèle's satisfaction. Her pleasure is instantly recognizable as such owing to the way in which it is filmed. Jump cuts between the two partners are used, focusing alternately on Auteuil's eyes and hands, and on Paradis's face and gyrating body. The jump cuts are gradually speeded up to signify mounting desire and the scene is accompanied by rapturous music. At the moment of 'climax', the image is rotated by 90 degrees, so that Paradis's standing figure appears to be horizontal, her arching back suggesting a woman's orgasm on a bed. One critic has described this as 'la belle scène d'orgasme derrière la voie ferrée'[10] (Rouyer 1999: 38–9).

10 'the beautiful orgasmic scene behind the railway'

While potentially problematic if read as the self-loathing resort of a desperate woman, an alternative reading of the scene is possible. The trust implied in giving oneself to the execution of a potentially fatal act suggests a means of representing the condition of the self-transcendental ethical subject, the 'one-that-steps-outside-of-itself'. A cynical reading which understands the knife-throwing ritual as exploitative, and as reinforcing rather than mobilizing the meaning of a male–female sexual power imbalance, relies on a prurient logic in which the presence of passion guarantees the sexual *and therefore sullied* nature of the scene and makes it dubious. This is close to what Žižek describes as the moral aporia of the postmodern condition whereby – quoting Hegel – 'evil is in the eye of the beholder' (Žižek 2000: 381).

My reading of the eroticization of death as bearing a potentially ethical agenda here is supported by the presence in the film of numerous other games involving acts risking death. Gabor and Adèle are shown repeatedly risking their lives in the pursuit of luck and chance (Gabor's 'pile ou face'[11] on the railway track; their nocturnal drive in absolute darkness, having extinguished the headlights of their car). These apparently childish and irresponsible acts constitute within the narrative a strategic siding with death as a rejection of the imperatives of socially sanctioned coupledom (marriage, repro-duction, reproducibility). The motifs of play and performativity that structure the narrative as a whole should not be read as indicating flippancy, superficiality or an absence of moral seriousness. Rather, they constitute a concerted attempt to reject the imperatives of outmoded forms of ethical interaction, and move the conceit of self-loss from a modern agenda to a postmodern one.

Just as *La Veuve de Saint-Pierre* juxtaposes two types of ethical discourse to demonstrate the dynamic of self-sacrifice, *La Fille sur le pont* exploits the *enjeu* of the 'jeu' – the game with chance played by two players – to construct a utopian model of postmodern ethical reciprocity. When Gabor and Adèle first meet, she is in despair. Her wild hair, tortured face and attitude of abjection convey a powerful image of otherness. However, Gabor fails initially to respond to the uniqueness of her plight. He assimilates her to the collection of similarly desperate girls he has met on the bridge previously, and co-

11 'heads or tails'

opts her suicidal drive for the purposes of his stage act. By the end of the film, the ethical attitudes of the characters have come full circle. Adèle connotes alterity for Gabor, communicated by the mystical qualities she possesses in relation to him (uncanny, death-defying luck, a telepathic connection, a sexuality that defies codification). They are thus inextricably bound together, but by bonds that are ephemeral rather than constricting. The closing scene mirrors the scene of their initial meeting: on a bridge, over the Bosphorous rather than the Seine, and instead of Adèle, it is Gabor who is contemplating ending his life. When Adèle arrives to 'rescue' him, it is by dint of a mystical power that has shown her where he is. The inclusion of these supernatural or fairy tale references, which are unexplained within the film, renders the encounter difficult to assimilate to codes of realism. Similarly, this time, Gabor does not attempt to understand Adèle's being on the bridge by means of comparison with others (the procession of suicidal women he has 'rescued' before) or by her use value (as his target). Their meeting is inexplicable and spontaneous and their continued union is founded on an ethical position of respect for each other's alterity that is not foreclosed in the diegetic space by reference to familiar endings (marriage, domesticity). Instead they are resolved to go 'n'importe où' (anywhere), so long as they are together. Leconte's agenda in debarring marriage and the family from his cinematic portrayal can be compared, as I have done earlier, to Blier's anti-bourgeois ideology. However, the difference is that Leconte's configurations, particularly in *La Fille sur le pont*, can be read as structured along the lines of a postmodern Levinasian parable, not so much a call to arms against society, as a knowing ethical response to the fragmentation of discourses of meaning.

In *La Fille sur le pont* the eroticization of death allows paradoxically for a celebration of life: discourses about death and eroticism are mobilized, so that death is maintained as a third term while both partners are allowed to live at the end. In this, it echoes Levinas's conception of love as described by Botting and Wilson:

> Love overcomes death precisely through risking it and thereby representing it in the movement that takes the self beyond itself towards the other. [...] It is thus a movement close to self-sacrifice, of giving of onself [sic] without recompense or return, a painful movement that, as Levinas observes, 'tears me from myself'. (Botting and Wilson 2002: 90)

*La Fille sur le pont* is revolutionary in its agenda as a love story for the twenty-first century. It pays lip service to the codes of romantic comedy, the love story and the *Liebestod*, but in such a way as to mobilize these codes, to make their meanings fluid and provisional. This film moves through an ironic dismantling of discursive constructions of idealized erotic love, only in order to demonstrate a transcendental principle which, stripped of the clichés of romance, is revealed as an ethics of love. While the closing scenes of *La Fille sur le pont* reveal a triumph of mutual respect in a relationship that has internalized the risk of metaphysical and physical death, the other films show the degree of sacrifice involved in limitless love or ceaseless watching over of the other.

By making gendered positions fluid in *La Fille sur le pont* and *La Veuve de Saint-Pierre*, and focusing on an equality of respect between the partners, Leconte frees femininity from its traditional association with death. Death is mobilized in these films as a powerful locus of otherness – the shadow of which inspires sexual ecstasy in the games with knives that form the central motif of *La Fille sur le pont*, and moral dread in the impending execution of *La Veuve de Saint-Pierre*. Death as a motif is linked to love and the couple in a manner reminiscent of the romantic motif of the *Liebestod* but – because of their profoundly ethical context – *La Fille sur le pont* and *La Veuve de Saint-Pierre* escape the straightforward romanticism of a film like *Le Mari de la coiffeuse*. Leconte mobilizes humanism and love as rhetorical weapons against cynicism in these films. Love is put in play, not in the sense of an inward-looking, insular longing for security with and through the other, but as a dynamic of risk. Apparent sentimentality is thereby harnessed as a discursive tool with which to relativize the hegemony of the 'cool', ethically sclerotic present.

## Along ethical lines: two men and a train

In *La Fille sur le pont*, the motif of train tracks was used to suggest the way in which chance and luck function as simultaneously arbitrary and contingent, and yet also of life-and-death import. In one scene, Gabor walks insouciantly along one fork of railway track. An oncoming train is shown in the distance approaching the fork. At the last minute, it veers off on to the other track and Gabor's life is spared.

When Adèle asks him frantically what he is doing, his answer is simple and delivered in calm tones: 'Je cherche ma voie'.[12] The symbolism of the railway as a locus of chance, contingency, encounter and transformation is expanded in Leconte's latest film *L'Homme du train*.

*L'Homme du train* unites the arch Lecontian hero Rochefort, as Manesquier, a lonely, retired school teacher living alone in a remote crumbling house, and the popular singer Johnny Halliday as Milan, an ageing bank robber, the eponymous traveller who arrives at Rochefort's small provincial town to carry out a 'job'. Manesquier offers hospitality to the stranger and a friendship develops between them, born of their admiration and appreciation of the other's differences (Manesquier lends Milan a comfortable pair of slippers and treats him to good food; Milan teaches Manesquier how to fire a gun). The narrative reaches its climax as the two men both face a day of reckoning: Manesquier's triple bypass operation and Milan's bank robbery.

*L'Homme du train* is self-deconstructive in its presentation of genre and characterization alike. One critic comments that in the film Leconte 'se plaît [...] à casser les mythes à mesure qu'il les esquisse'[13] (Rouyer 2002: 220). This is most obviously seen in the figure of Milan, the would-be criminal hero of the western genre. The photograph of himself that he proudly shows to Manesquier, supposedly taken in the Nevada desert, is later revealed to have been taken at a circus. This mismatch between aspiration and actuality is repeatedly reinforced in the shots that juxtapose the banality and everyday detail of provincial life (the regulars in the café-bar which Manesquier frequents; the annoying girl in the baker's shop who repeats her catch phrase 'et avec ceci?'[14] perpetually and tirelessly) with Milan's glamorous performance of filmic masculinity (denims, leathers, moustache and gun). The gaps in Milan's performance of the stereotype to which he aspires is paradigmatic of Leconte's project in these late films of demystifying the constructions of subjectivity that pass for the innateness of identities.

Moreover, this film, whose key thematic preoccupations can be said to be maturation, demystification and reflection on the past, is extremely self-aware in terms of its intertexts with other films in

12 'I'm looking for my way'
13 'gets pleasure from destroying myths as soon as he has sketched them'
14 'anything else with that?'

Leconte's *œuvre*, enacting its subject matter in its very construction. *L'Homme du train* is the most emotionally sombre film in Leconte's repertoire since *Le Mari de la coiffeuse* (also scripted by Claude Klotz) and it is not coincidental that it contains a direct intertextual reference to this film. In one scene, Rochefort enters a barber's shop and has his hair cut by Maurice Chevit, who played the role of Monsieur Alphonse, the retired gay hairdresser, in *Le Mari de la coiffeuse*. Thus, in these frames, the film seems to perform a repetition of Rochefort's earlier incarnation, suggesting reflection upon the accrued representations of subjectivity and masculinity within the Lecontian corpus. Yet, the very boldness of this revisitation of earlier territory in a film which calls the earlier text's ideology into question suggests not the melancholic, claustrophobic interiority of *Le Mari de la coiffeuse* but a ludic allusion to earlier incarnations and a concomitant signalling of their arbitrariness.

What is more, the emotional tone and structure of the film evoke not only repetition and nostalgia, but also the potential of futurity and 'what if?'. The film ends on a semantic puzzle, suggesting at once circularity and completion, and yet, simultaneously, enigma, open-endedness and mystery. As both protagonists lie apparently dying – Manesquier from a failed surgical operation, Milan from a shoot-out – we cut to scenes of Milan returning to his friend's house to take up the life of the retired school teacher, while Manesquier prepares to board the train on which Milan arrived, to seek out the limitless adventures his previous life of comfort and confinement had precluded.

These images have uncertain status within the narrative. We cannot be sure whether they are the fantasies of dying men; examples of futile wish-fulfilment for the identificatory pleasure of the audience; or a flash-forward to future lives if the characters somehow survive their critical plights. However, the imaginary power of the closing scene is considerable, as it offers a filmic representation of being in a mode that suspends the generic and conventional certainties of realist narrative that would demand an answer to the either/or of the dream/reality binarism. The hesitant uncertainty of the denouement allows the film to attain the status of a speculation on aesthetic conventions and discourses of being.

The 'being' put under scrutiny in *L'Homme du train* might be more properly designated 'becoming' in the sense that Gilles Deleuze understands the term. 'Becoming' is a mode of experience that comes about as the result of an encounter between two parties. The encounter leads each entity to undergo change, but without being transformed into the other. The relationship described is not straightforwardly one of mimicry or mirroring, for that would imply fixed original identities capable of being 'copied'. Rather, the transformation is one of unstable flux, a perpetual movement-towards-being brought about by the affecting presence of the other. (To thematize this movement, Deleuze quotes Rimbaud's famous dictum 'Je est un autre'[15] (Deleuze 1985: 199).) The impossible fantasy ending of *L'Homme du train* – a movement towards a new life for each protagonist from within mortality – describes the impossibility of ever *changing into* the other, while celebrating retroactively the ethical transformative power of the encounter.

Seen through a Levinasian lens, *L'Homme du train* thematizes the power of the face to effect self-reflection. It dramatizes a coming-to-consciousness through an encounter with the other. The characters in the film relativize their own subjectivity and are profoundly affected by *difference*. For one critic, the film stands as an ethical allegory with considerable import for our age: 'nous sommes tous des Milan et des Manesquier'[16] (Rouyer 2002: 221).

## Some concluding remarks

My readings of Leconte's most recent films in this chapter have tried to show parallels and similarities with a strand of ethical thinking in contemporary Continental thought that 'displac[es] the conventional concerns of ethics with moral agency, with rights and justice, on to the singularity of the demand of responsibility towards the ultimate unknowability of "the other"' (Botting and Wilson 2002: 4). This has not been in the interests of arguing that a narrative film, much less a romantic comedy, can stage an ethical encounter *for the viewer* (i.e. that the faces on the screen are manifestations of the face in the way in which Levinas conceives of it). The mediated nature of the cinematic spectacle and the question of authorial intent mean that the encounter is never the spontaneous, arresting moment of ethical interrogation described by Levinas. What I am proposing, however, is that the logic

15 '"I" is an other'
16 'we are all Milan and Manesquier'

of Leconte's filming of the encounter between, for example, Adèle and Gabor or Manesquier and Milan, is extremely suggestive of a strand of philosophical enquiry that is seldom recognized as a critical intertext within cinema studies. Leconte's films have rarely been considered in the light of such a 'serious' meta-filmic agenda. Love as a transcendental principle, beyond notions of appropriation, interpretation and objectification of the one by the other, suggests the utopian element that underlies much of Leconte's work, despite its apparently cynical tone.

Moreover, a postmodern Levinasian reading of Leconte suggests a strategy for understanding the ethical potential of humour and parody that I alluded to in chapter 2. Comedy undermines the ego's ambitions of sovereignty; it allows for a splintering and fragmenting of the fixed 'I' of modern subjectivity. Thus, the techniques of humour, parody and pastiche that run through and draw together the whole of Leconte's body of films can be read as operating in the service of a radical ethical and postmodern agenda that could not be imagined if one read the films only in the context of local political or social realities, that is, in the context of a modern ethical mode.

### References

Bauman, Zygmunt (1993), *Postmodern Ethics*, Oxford, Blackwell.

Botting, Fred and Wilson, Scott (2002), *The Tarantinian Ethics*, London, Sage.

Cohen, Richard A. (ed.) (1986), 'Dialogue with Emmanuel Levinas', in *Face to Face With Levinas*, Albany NY, Suny, 13–33.

Davis, Colin (2000), *Ethical Issues in Twentieth-Century French Fiction: Killing the Other*, Basingstoke and London, Macmillan.

Deleuze, Gilles (1985), *L'Image-temps*, Paris, Minuit.

Downing, Lisa (2002), 'Between Men and Women; Beyond Heterosexuality: Limits and Possibilities of the Erotic in Lynne Stopkewich's *Kissed* and Patrice Leconte's *La Fille sur le pont*', *Romance Studies*, 20: 1, June, 29–40.

Levinas, Emmanuel ([1961] 1969), *Totality and Infinity: An Essay on Exteriority*, translated by Alphonso Lingis, Pittsburgh, Duquesne University Press.

Marshall, Bill (forthcoming), 'The French Atlantic', in *Encyclopaedia of French-American Relations*, ed. Bill Marshall, Oxford and Santa Barbara, ABC-Clio.

Rouyer, Philippe (1999), 'La Vie sur un fil de couteau', *Positif*, May, 38–9.

Rouyer, Philippe (2002), 'L'Homme du train', *Positif*, October, 220–1.

Thirard, Paul Louis and Tobin, Yann (2002), 'Patrice Leconte: De Vanessa Paradis à *Rue des plaisirs*', *Positif*, February, 28–34.

Vincendeau, Ginette (2000), '*La Fille sur le pont*', *Sight and Sound*, June, 44.

Witt, Mike (2000), '*La Veuve de Saint-Pierre*', *Sight and Sound*, September, 56–7.

Žižek, Slavoj (1993), *Tarrying with the Negative: Kant, Hegel and the Critique of Ideology*, Durham NC, Duke University Press.

Žižek, Slavoj (2000), *The Ticklish Subject: The Absent Centre of Political Ontology*, London and New York, Verso.

# Conclusion

> Leconte [...] is best compared to one of those studio cobblers and
> cabinet makers of 1930s and 1940s Hollywood: the kind Polonius
> would have liked, who could produce 'comedy, history, pastoral,
> pastoral-comical, historical-pastoral, tragical-historical, tragical-
> comical-historical-pastoral'. (Lennon 2003: 38)

In a short tribute to Woody Allen written for *Positif* in 1994, Leconte
acknowledges – and celebrates – the eclecticism which has characterized
his cinematic influences and tastes. At the same time, he highlights
the ethical problem inherent in paying homage to any given actor or
director:

> [L]a moindre des choses serait de rendre hommage à Jean Gabin. Mais
> ce serait passer sous silence Groucho Marx. Ou bien alors parler de
> Miou-Miou qui est celle qui, depuis toujours, me touche et m'émeut.
> Mais ce serait oublier Michelle Pfeiffer, Judith Godrèche, Katharine
> Hepburn, Sandrine Bonnaire, Julia Roberts, Fanny Ardant...[1] (Leconte
> 1994: 71)

In his eagerness to do justice to all those artists who have touched or
impressed him, Leconte crosses nationality and generation, before
finally expressing his admiration for the iconic Jewish-American
tragic-comic director and actor. This reluctance, this restless, irritable
inability to commit to any one discernable position or to follow any

---

1 'It would be all too easy to pay homage to Jean Gabin. But that would mean
  saying nothing about Groucho Marx. Or else to talk about Miou-Miou, who has
  always touched me and moved me. But that would mean forgetting about
  Michelle Pfeiffer, Judith Godrèche, Katharine Hepburn, Sandrine Bonnaire,
  Julia Roberts, Fanny Ardant ...'

singular influence is perhaps at the heart of Leconte's diversity as a filmmaker.

We have seen that this diversity is part of what irritates critics about Leconte, and has led to a dismissal of his filmic project as lacking seriousness. Leconte's refusal to profess an *engagement* (commitment) to a single filmic genre, style, social project or political agenda is often dismissed as revelatory of a frivolous or adolescent lack of gravity. However, to see Leconte as unconcerned by questions of ethics is to misread both the director's self-deprecating rhetoric and his films. Just as he refuses to capitulate to the demands of any given generic mode, so Leconte's political position is precisely characterized by an awareness of the ethical problem of committing to any one cause, movement, moment or position.

However, my assertion that Leconte should be understood as a consummately ethical filmmaker is a controversial one for several reasons. Within academic film criticism, theories of ethics tend to be discussed in relation primarily to documentary filmmaking, rather than narrative cinema.[2] In contradistinction to Jean Rouch's ethnographic project, or a documentary film which attempts to memorialize the horror of collective trauma (e.g. Alain Resnais's evocation of Nazi concentration camps in *Nuit et brouillard* (1955)), Leconte's narrative films, made with the aim of seducing and entertaining the audience, may indeed seem to lack in *gravitas*. These narrative films do not even represent, directly or allegorically, events of world history or politics, one might object. Indeed, Leconte has made many statements, some of which are cited in this book, to the effect that the realities of politics and history do not interest him as subject matter and that his films serve instead as vehicles to convey 'la rêverie', 'un monde inventé' and 'l'imaginaire'[3] (Leconte 2000: 48). It is a tempting 'common sense' assumption to propose that a body of films that takes its bearings in the realms of fantasy or the banal everyday must be a less ethically valid project than one which treats the great social and political questions of an age. However, as I argued in chapter 5, postmodern theories of ethics allow for a slightly different perspective on this question. Leconte's films relocate ethical questions away from

2 A good example is Sarah Cooper's recent article, which reads Jean Rouch's documentary filmmaking in the light of Levinasian ethics and Deleuzian theories of becoming (Cooper 2003).

3 'day dreams, an invented world, the imaginary'

the body politic and into an imaginary world of intersubjective chal-lenges, dilemmas and interactions. This abstraction from social reality means that considerations of power, of responsibility and of sacrifice attain in Leconte's cinema the status of philosophical concepts.

Moreover, analyses of documentary filmmaking and political narrative cinema focus on the inevitable problem encountered by these art forms regarding the question of mimesis, or the possibility of neutral representation. The attempt to convey objective, unmedi-ated reality on celluloid is a problematic project, as a filmed spectacle that is chosen, composed, framed, edited and cut is as far from the lived reality it purports to transmit as one could imagine. Similarly, films which treat the subject matter of collective trauma, such as holocaust the documentary films *Nuit et brouillard* and *Shoah* (Lanz-mann 1985) confront the tension between, on the one hand, an imperative to represent an event – thereby gaining narrative mastery of it – and, on the other hand, the ethical exigency not to reduce or violate the integrity of an unrepresentable experience of trauma.

In the light of this understanding, Leconte's rejection of the imperative to provide *any* testimony or direct political commentary can be read as an ethical act in its own right. By doggedly and osten-tatiously pursuing 'the personal' in the most extreme way, Leconte's cinema highlights the ubiquity of that category and, by extension, highlights the difficulty of any attempt at directorial neutrality. Secondly, Leconte refuses the potentially exploitative exposure of the real of human suffering, and opts instead to put on screen a politics of the imaginary.

The ambiguity which characterizes the vexed question of Leconte's *engagement* is paralleled by the difficulty of discerning whether his cinema can be properly described as an *auteur*ist one. The question of the extent to which Leconte's cinema rejects and yet, at moments, paradoxically upholds the notion of a directorial vision is one which has preoccupied my readings throughout this book. While refusing to make several films in the same genre, privileged themes, narrative devices and character types nevertheless recur. The exploration of Leconte's most recent work *L'Homme du train* in the previous chapter offers a neat insight into this paradox. The mature reassessment of earlier themes and the reappearance of familiar figures, both diegetic archetypes and prized actors in *L'Homme du train* lends credence to the notion of a consistent Lecontian universe; a universe of interaction, characterized by the import of the chance encounter, ethical challenges and inevitable loss. This consistency paradoxically exists alongside the diversity and disparity of Leconte's work, both generically and in terms of critically perceived 'quality'.

The existence of a recognizable filmic universe that crosses and joins the individual works, then, places Leconte in the camp of *auteur*ist cinema. Like Truffaut's Antoine Doinel cycle, it is possible to trace the progress of recognizable figures through the course of Leconte's cinema. However, rather than following the fortunes of one onscreen character, readable as a straightforward directorial alter ego, Leconte's cinema offers a prismatic lens on to various aspects of human subjectivity. The repeated recasting of certain actors (Michel Blanc, Jean Rochefort) does suggest a male centre of subjectivity with which there is strong directorial identification, a fact that is corroborated by Leconte's own account. However, the notion of the stable onscreen subject as a central figure of identification is not the whole story here. By casting Rochefort and other onscreen alter egos in a series of roles that disrupt naturalized myths of masculinity (a mechanism I have termed in chapter 3 the revelation of the masculine masquerade), Leconte sidesteps the lure of the Doinel model, whereby the iconic status of the fictional filmic character provides a univocal, masculine vision which neatly parallels and eclipses the director's.

Similarly, despite the fact that many of Leconte's films are criticized for being constructed from the viewpoint of the heterosexual male, with the female characters being on the whole less rich and complex, the strategic use of stars in Leconte's later career does nuance his presentation of the sexes and the meanings of gender. The reappearance of Vanessa Paradis – transformed from the archetypal daughter of *Une chance sur deux* to the maverick Adèle in *La Fille sur le pont* – suggests a self-aware project of revision; an attempt to move outside of a tradition of ideologically dubious representations of women. Similarly, the reincarnation of the figure of Mathilde, the suicidal hairdresser, in the personage of Adèle, who survives her own postmodern fairytale, suggests a progressive undermining of stereotypical gender roles and an awareness of the cultural contingency of performances of identity.

Thus, despite some elements of consistency in Leconte's presentation of subjectivity and relationality, and despite his – at first glance – conservative vision of sexuality as heterosexual and phallic, his experimental play with identity via the manipulation of actor-texts, as well as his celebrated generic experimentation, undermine the threat of univocal *auteur*ism and prevent his vision becoming monolithic.

This embracing of multiplicity extends to – or perhaps has at its heart – Leconte's commitment to collaboration. The title of Leconte's autobiography, *Je suis un imposteur*, reflects directly an impatience with the notion of cinematic authorship and the cult of directorial celebrity. Leconte asserts that a film is the product of a community of creative talents including writers, camera operators, set design teams and actors, as well as the director (see my 'Conversation with Patrice Leconte' in the appendix of this book). Similarly, *Patrice, Leconte et les autres* (Chantier and Lemeunier 2001), the only existing published volume about Leconte's cinema in French (at the time of going to press), focuses – in its choice of title and its contents – on the collaborative nature of Leconte's cinematography. It addresses the important part played by such names as Christian Fechner, Michel Blanc, Claude Klotz and Patrick Dewolf in the creation of a filmic universe – however riven and paradoxical – that can be designated Lecontian. The title is, of course, also a pun on Claude Sautet's *Vincent, François, Paul ... et les autres* (1974). Sautet, along with Blier, are names often associated with Leconte, as the three directors are known to focus in their films on male friendship and the changing role of masculinity in the second half of the twentieth century. This implicit alignment of Leconte with the projects of other directors suggests a second, and equally important, interpretation of 'les autres'.

'Les autres', then, may designate as well the community of contemporary film directors of which Leconte is a part, even if his role in this community is ambiguous and often difficult to define. In both his filmmaking and in his public interventions regarding the state of the industry Leconte pursues an often unpopular but always thought-provoking agenda. By his refusal to specialize in one genre, by his obsessive focus on the spheres of the everyday and the personal, and by his repeated juxtaposing and blending of high and low cultural forms, Leconte's cinema can be seen to stand in satirical opposition to some of the purist aesthetic and social obsessions of the French cinema industry and its critics. This gentle mode of refusal, which, perhaps more than any other single feature, entirely characterizes Leconte, makes him a significant and subversive name in the canon of contemporary French directors.

This conclusion can be only a provisional one, insofar as we have every reason to believe that Leconte's filmmaking career is far from over, and that its future may be as eclectic as its past. Thus, the most appropriate revisionist reading and viewing gesture that needs to be made with regard to Leconte's cinema is one which seeks to appreciate its paradoxical qualities and the fruitful tensions it embodies. It is simultaneously recognizable as a consistent directorial project, which gains in complexity and maturity over the years, while also bearing analysis as a body of work that is open, multiple and generous: in the meanings and interpretations it offers, as well as in its practices of production.

## References

Chantier, Pascal and Lemeunier, Jean-Charles (2001), *Patrice, Leconte et les autres*, Paris, Séguier.

Cooper, Sarah (2003), 'Other than Becoming: Jean Rouch and the Ethics of *Les Maîtres fous*', *French Studies*, 56: 4, 483–94.

Leconte, Patrice (1994), 'Patrice Leconte: S'il n'en reste qu'un ...', *Positif*, June, 71.

Leconte, Patrice (2000), *Je suis un imposteur*, Paris, Flammarion.

Lennon, Peter (2003), 'Don't Shoot the Director', *Guardian Weekend*, 29 May, 38–40.

# Appendix: conversation with Patrice Leconte, 9 February 2003[1]

Lisa Downing: The title of your autobiography intrigues me. Why are you an impostor? Or is it just a joke?

Patrice Leconte: Of course, it is a bit of a joke to create a catchy title. When the publisher convinced me to write a book of this sort, I was looking for a title and I didn't want to say something like 'The Story of My Life', because I thought that was far too pretentious. It had to be rather eye-catching, while still reflecting a certain reality. Indeed, the idea that I am an impostor does move around my head on a regular basis. What I mean by it is that when one says to a painter or a novelist, for instance, 'Your painting is magnificent' or 'Your book is magnificent', this comment refers to the artist's work only. A filmmaker, by contrast, brings together the work of many different people, who are all talented. Alone, one means nothing. Alone, the filmmaker doesn't have talent. Of course, he may be talented, but at the end of the day, when a film is successful, when it receives good reviews, when one reaps the rewards, when someone says: 'I love your film, Mr Leconte', it is still being said to a single person. Yet that person didn't do it all by himself. I always say to myself: 'This isn't right. There are so many of them'. There is the set designer who is so talented, there is the editor who was wonderful, there is the writer who had a sensational idea, the actors, the lighting team, all of those people ... So the idea of being an impostor is both true and false, but it mainly refers to the feeling of sometimes receiving compliments that need be shared with many different people.

LD: I understand. It is a very modest notion.

1 This conversation was transcribed by Dany Nobus and translated from the French by Dany Nobus and Lisa Downing. It is reproduced with the kind permission of Patrice Leconte

PL: But it is not false modesty. I have never thought 'me, me, me'. My talent, if I have it, is to be successful in bringing together various things, so that, at the end of the day, the talent of all these people together may generate successful films. From time to time it doesn't work, I make a mistake, and the films aren't successful at all. But, there you go: one is never alone when it comes to making films.

LD: But you are still young. Why did you decide to write your autobiography at this stage of your life?

PL: I didn't really choose to do it. A charming guy from Flammarion, who edits a collection of books, said to me one day: 'I would like to meet you. I really like your films. Let's have lunch together'. And when I met him, he said: 'I wanted to see you because I thought it would be interesting if you were to write down some anecdotes, some memories'. And I said: 'I am not sure. I think it's much better to do that when one is slightly older'. But he was insistent. And, then, during lunch he prompted me to recall things that had happened when I shot my films, encounters with actors etc., and I found myself getting into it. I told him things about my profession, about my films. And he said to me: 'This is exactly what I want'. So I finally agreed and said: 'Look, I shall try. If I succeed and it is interesting, you can publish it. If at the end of three or four pages I don't succeed and the whole thing is a washout, we shall stop the project'. Well, it was summertime and I left for the countryside. I wasn't working on a film at the time and every day I thought about what I was going to write during the evening. And, then, when the evening came and it was cooler, I would write this book. In September I gave it to him. And he told me: 'It's interesting. We shall publish it'. And there it is.

LD: So it wasn't your own decision. It wasn't a decision that you would have taken.

PL: Never, never. Obviously, I might decide one day to write a play, or to write a series of short stories, or to write things that are not directly related to my profession. I can make that decision, but the decision to write a book on my work, my itinerary, my films, would never have occurred to me.

LD: You make some interesting claims in the book, though. At one point you mention that during your youth, as a student at the IDHEC, you weren't interested in politics at all and that the events of May '68 left you rather indifferent. Is that true or is it a cynical remark?

PL: It is of course a bit cynical. It is a form of humour, but at the same time I have never felt like a person – neither a person nor a filmmaker – who is really, deliberately militant or politically committed. My own form of militancy is much more related to humankind. If I do militate for a better world, it would be through my films, through the happiness one tries to instil, through the eyes of the spectator that one tries to open so that they see the world differently, so that they are more in love with their partners ... It wouldn't be all that bad if one were to succeed in it. Even if it only made people more tolerant, more aware even. My commitment is much more humanist than political, definitely. But I try to play my music in such a way that people feel uplifted, rather than being brought down. When I say it in this way, it sounds like 'mission impossible', but I shall always remember the words of Wim Wenders. One day, when he was the president of the jury at the Cannes festival, he was asked: 'Why do you make your films?' And he said: 'I make my films to make the world a better place'. And I said to myself: 'Well, this guy is clearly no fool'. It is a bit pretentious, I suppose. But in the end I think he is right, because one can indeed make the world a better place in this way. And one isn't even obliged to make films with the explicit intention of making the world a better place or stirring a revolution. One can gently slip some interesting ideas into people's minds. Hence, I have never been militant, or committed politically. I try to live my life and make my films more gently and more humanely. And politics pisses me off, enormously. I don't understand a thing that politicians say. They are all interchangeable. One does not know who to believe; who is a liar and who is telling the truth.

LD: Perhaps this brings us to *Ridicule*, a film in which you mock the political need to persuade and to convince, without any consideration for morality.

PL: Yes, *Ridicule* is a very good example of what I feel. The hero of *Ridicule*, Ponceludon de Malavoy, comes from the provinces, just like me. And he has an ideal. Of course, I myself do not have a humanitarian ideal. If I have an ideal at all, it is with regard to filmmaking. But this boy has an ideal. He arrives at Versailles and he knocks on the door of power, but he doesn't obtain anything. The boy is authentic. He has a project. He needs some money but he doesn't get anything. For me, this is a reflection of how I think. I have the impression that when one calls upon politicians these days, one never gets a good answer. But I am saying this in front of a person who agrees with me.

LD: For me, there is a strong ethical drive in your films. But it doesn't concern, let's say, a 'local' ethics, nor a question of politics, as you have said. It is much more concerned with encounters between people, with what you observe in everyday life when people meet one another, and which requires a certain authentic response, an ethical response, which sometimes your characters are able to give and sometimes they are incapable of giving. I find this dimension quite touching.

PL: I am very moved by what you have just said. It is true that the essence of my inspiration and what nourishes my imagination in the films I make is the everyday, only the everyday. Because one can learn a lot from observing people leading their lives. That is how one learns to see and to think differently. 'And this is how people live': it is a song by Leo Ferré, isn't it ... Well, this is what interests me. To ask the question: 'Isn't it possible to live a bit better than this? Isn't it possible to be better in the way we look at the other too?' It is not always evident in all my films, because I don't want it to be overwhelming as a message. For the notion of 'message' is also a heavy burden. But it is definitely what animates me.

LD: I understood you correctly, then?

PL: Yes, and it touches me, because sometimes I am told: 'I don't understand what you have tried to do' in a given film. So it makes me happy that you say that.

LD: I am pleased about that ... You have made several films, such as *Tandem* and *L'Homme du train*, about men who are struggling to find out what it means to be a 'man' within contemporary society. In your opinion, are twentieth- and twenty-first-century men facing an identity crisis?

PL: Well, yes ... I would want to avoid talking about myself all the time, but I guess one always puts oneself emotionally within one's films. We are never estranged from our own films. Actually, sometimes we can be strangers to our films, but it's unfortunate if that happens. One should not make a film if one is really distanced from it. The big question: 'How can one be a man these days – a husband, a lover, a father, quite simply a man, a man among other men' is a question which always comes back to me. But it is a question which always comes back because it is triggered by a lucid and very sincere observation. I think that at every stage of life, at each stage of equal ages, women are always more mature than men. Take five-year-old girls and five-year-old boys. Well, five-year-old boys are very stupid and the girls are already more interesting. At the age of 10, 20, 50 even, women always seem more interesting than men to me. I think there is always more that society as a whole could learn from women. I don't mean that as a sort of idolatry, but we men can learn a lot from women if we are able to keep our eyes open. For this reason too, I say to myself that this must make a man's life more complicated. If one believes that women are more interesting people than men, then it must obviously make it difficult to live as a man. In any case, it is true that the men in my films are asking themselves questions such as: 'How can one live and make as few mistakes as possible? How can one live in a more or less dignified fashion? How can one assume one's own cowardice? How can one assume one's defects, in full awareness of them?' All of this keeps me busy. It doesn't keep me awake, but it does keep coming back.

LD: And at a certain moment in your career you made a number of films in succession about masculine friendship. More recently, you have concentrated rather on the relationship between men and women. What inspired you to make this change?

PL: The first films I made were very much designed to put things on the road. I deliberately made comedies, *Les Bronzés* etc., with perhaps lower emotional stakes, one could say. I was less involved in them. Subsequently, when I started making slightly more personal films, which touched me more closely, I didn't think myself sufficiently mature, both in the films I wanted to make and in my ideas, to stage important female characters. *Tandem*, which was the first more personal film, was about two men in a car on the road. Afterwards, there was *Monsieur Hire* and in this film Monsieur Hire is behind the window and the woman is on the other side of the courtyard. Hence, there was desire, but it couldn't travel across ... And then things started to clarify themselves a bit with *Le Mari de la coiffeuse*, because here it really is about a man and a woman, alone and in love, in a hairdresser's salon. I approached it very gently. It wasn't conscious on my part. I am saying it today with hindsight. And then, afterwards, I succeeded in staging female characters and got a great deal of pleasure out of working with actresses, as opposed to working only with actors. I started to feel at ease. And I managed to enjoy making the other films. I amused myself drawing very important, strong female characters. And then I forgot about them again just for the duration of one film, because my most recent film, *L'Homme du train*, only concerns two men. I went back to the buddy movie or, if not buddies, then at least a certain masculine complicity. In the next film, it will be a man and a woman again. So now I feel that I am walking about freely.

LD: Of all your films, the one I get on with the least is *Le Parfum d'Yvonne*. What does this film mean to you?

PL: *Le Parfum d'Yvonne* is a strange adventure ... The origins of *Le Parfum d'Yvonne* are as follows: I harboured the idea, the desire, to make a film in which eroticism would be quite manifest, strong, open, deliberate. But I didn't want to make an erotic film all by myself, telling the entire story myself. When I came across this novel by Modiano, *Villa triste*, I felt that between the lines there was a slightly outdated eroticism that was nonetheless absolutely charming and which could be expressed in the images of a film, and which it was even possible to take a step further. I could already sense in the book this scent, this direction. And then I accepted this proposition from a producer who said to me: 'Have you read this?' And at that point I hadn't read the book by Modiano, but when I read it I said to myself: 'Well, perhaps this is an opportunity to follow a new direction, just for the duration of one film, which is more deliberately erotic, sensuous'. And in the beginning, I made the film for these reasons. Later I was animated by other motivations, notably the character of René Meinthe, played by Jean-Pierre Marielle, who is this detached, decadent homosexual figure. I recognized that I started the film inspired by an interest in the sensuous or the erotic, and that gradually I developed a passion for the character of Meinthe, played by Marielle. But all of this resulted in a film made for bad reasons. And the result is a film which is hard to situate. But, strangely enough, I know people who are infatuated with it.

LD: It is certainly a very strange film.

PL: I don't watch my own films every night, but when I saw *Le Parfum d'Yvonne* again some time ago, I thought it was a rather vain film, a bit useless – although I am not sure whether films should be useful – but even today I think that *Le Parfum d'Yvonne* contains moments that I believe to be very successful at evoking a certain kind of distress, the twilight side of our emotional lives. There are very shallow elements in the film, without interest, and then there are much more serious things, close to vertigo, which I really liked. But, look, there are successful and unsuccessful films. It is really bizarre, because when you started talking and you said: 'There is a film I don't understand etc.', I didn't think you were going to mention *Le Parfum d'Yvonne*. I thought about another film. I thought you were going to say this about *Tango*.

LD: Oh no, I admire *Tango* immensely.

PL: You know, there is something bizarre about my films. Those people who like what I do – one cannot put everyone into that category, of course, thankfully – tell me: 'Well, really, the film I like the most is *Monsieur Hire*'. And then there are others who say: 'I like your films a lot. For me, the best one is *Les Grands Ducs*.' And so there is the club *Les Grands Ducs* and the club of people who prefer *Monsieur Hire*. There is the club *Le Mari de la coiffeuse*. There are people who admire *Tango*. There are people who adore *Le Parfum d'Yvonne*, and for others it is *La Veuve de Saint-Pierre*, etc.

LD: ... ah, the famous Lecontian eclecticism ...

PL: Yes, perhaps because my films are all so different, people attach themselves to one or another of them.

LD: It strikes me that you are almost the only French filmmaker of your generation who doesn't seem to respect, or to be limited by, generic constraints. This is a quality that I appreciate very much in your films.

PL: That is something I enjoy very much. I adore exploring in order to see what will happen ... I think that's the best analogy for it. When you go out for a walk, in the countryside, in a landscape you are not familiar with, along small paths, suddenly you say to yourself: 'Do I need to go right or left?' And then: 'What shall I do at the crossroads'. Somehow, though, you always find your way home, because there is the sun to help you know where you are. I don't think that when you are out exploring you can really get lost. There are plenty of landmarks. There will always be a road to take you back home and you will be back by night fall. But it is about exploring without knowing too much in advance.

LD: It is a kind of wandering about (*flânerie*), then.

PL: Yes, it is intuitive. And I prefer that to the notion of a GPS [global positioning system] for cars that tells you: 'Take the first street to the right. Take the second street to the left. At the roundabout...'. GPS systems are quite clever when it comes to directing cars, but not for making films. I love to let myself go at the whim of the projects that I encounter and the ideas that enter my head.

LD: Do you think that this might be the reason why your films are sometimes misunderstood, not very well received? The difficulty one has in putting you into a category?

PL: Yes, perhaps, but in all honesty, I really want to claim this right to freedom, even when this freedom takes me from time to time in the direction of incoherence. I don't care.

LD: OK, a big question: as far as the love between individuals is concerned, as far as peace between the peoples and religions of the world, are you pessimistic or optimistic? It is not always clear from your films, at least not for me.

PL: I would love to be an optimist but alas an optimist these days is not a realist. Above all, an optimist is a dreamer. And this is what I try to preserve within myself. You know, I really believe that for the world to become a better place, there is one single magic formula that we might apply. For me, this formula is the 'respect for the other'. If one were to respect the other, there would be no famine anymore, countries would no longer be at war, there would be no racism anymore. All the ailments of our planet would be regulated, if each of us were to respect the other. And when I think this to myself, it is tempting to say: 'Oh, then it's incredibly easy'. But that would be the optimism of the dreamer. I myself try to slip this idea into my films, as best as I can, and also into my personal life, if possible, obviously. But I find it hard, because the notion hasn't made a lot of progress. And it nonetheless appears to me as a very simple thing. I can seriously say that I thought about this question for a very long time and I came to this simple notion of the respect for the other; these four words, which clearly don't seem to entail all that much. No kidding, it regulates everything. If you respect the other and you are a petroleum magnate you won't dump oil on the beaches. If you respect the other, you won't underpay the people who are doing important work ... etc. Hence, this is the magic formula. One can put it in gilded letters.

LD: I think you are right.

PL: I am really worried, though, because I don't have the impression that we are making much progress in that direction. And sometimes I worry and say to myself: 'I have kids and I hope that they won't be too unhappy, and the children of my children, what sort of world will they have?' But on the other hand, if one is to avoid having very negative thoughts and jumping from the balcony screaming 'I want to live!', one has to ask: 'Has there ever been a time when it wasn't so? Was there ever an era when we didn't have these black thoughts and ask these questions about the future, about peace between men and women, about peace in the world in general?' And we do continue to live today. Hasn't the world only known more sombre tomorrows? I have the impression that the world has never had anything *but* more sombre tomorrows. And, nonetheless, we are still here.

LD: It's true. We have survived the most unthinkable of things.

PL: We have survived religious wars. We have survived the most devastating diseases. We have survived famine. We have survived the Ice Age. We have survived incredible things.

LD: Apparently, we haven't learnt very much though.

PL: It's true. We haven't drawn many lessons from it. But I am not sure whether the phenomenon is accelerating now or not. Disrespect for the planet, all those who live now and say: 'We will be dead tomorrow and therefore we can't be bothered', disrespect for future generations. One has the impression that it is becoming more inhumane.

LD: Do you have a project under way at the moment?

PL: Yes, I am starting to shoot on 7 April [2003], a new film. I like the scenario very much. It is an original screenplay, written by a writer with whom I have worked before. The film is called *Confidences trop intimes*. We are still looking for an English title, because one day the film will be released in England and it is not easy to translate.

LD: What is it about?

PL: It is a very simple story that starts almost like a Hitchcock film. A young woman who isn't very well, who has sorrows, problems, decides to go and see a therapist.

LD: A bit like Adèle in *La Fille sur le pont*. Is it a similar type of character?

PL: Adèle is quite different, actually. One doesn't really know to whom Adèle is speaking at the beginning.

LD: It's true. I took it to be a mental health professional, but perhaps not.

PL: Yes, it's very stylized, on purpose. One doesn't know to whom she is speaking. And, in fact, she is speaking on a reality show, on television. She testifies ... I'm sure you have this in England, programmes where people say: 'Well, I have problems with my husband and other things ...'. Anyway, a young woman who is troubled decides to see a therapist.

It is an important decision because one is generally suspicious about these people, but she decides to do it. She is a bit fragile. She takes the name from a register. And she says: 'Right, it's close to where I work, so I shall take that one'. She makes an appointment. She arrives at the building. She takes the elevator to the sixth floor. And the attendant has told her: 'It's on the sixth floor, third door on the right'. She arrives on the sixth floor, but she takes the third door on the left, not on the right. She calls and she meets someone who is not a therapist but a financial advisor who doesn't realize that she wants to see a therapist. And she starts telling him about her problems. When he realizes that she has got the wrong person, he doesn't dare to tell her. She continues to talk to him and so suddenly, he, a man, is made privy, is given access to a woman's confidential secrets that are very intimate. No man, apart from mental health professionals ...

LD: ... and priests ...

PL: And priests, yes, and hairdressers ... Thus, he is very disturbed by this young woman, by the secrets that she trusts him with. And when after two sessions, for he doesn't dare to tell her that he is not a mental health professional, she realizes the truth, she comes back to him and says: 'I know you are not a psychologist'. And she continues to see him.

LD: That's great.

PL: I hope so.

LD: When will it come out?

PL: In about a year, in France.

LD: I look forward to it.

.

# Filmography

## Short films

### 1962

*Le Tour du monde de Monsieur Jones* (animation) (16 mm) 12 mins
*Les Voisins* (8 mm) 20 mins

### 1963

*Schweppes* (8 mm) 2'30 mins
*Incomprissionisme* (16 mm) 20 mins
*Corrida* (8 mm) 3'30 mins
*La Chute* (animation) (16 mm) 4 mins

### 1964

*Antoine* (16 mm) 20 mins
*Morte-Carne* (8 mm) 2 mins
*Sans gamelles ni bidons* (16 mm) 13 mins

### 1965

*Monsieur Ploum* (16 mm) 22 mins
*Les Dieux au goutte-à-goutte* (16 mm) 14 mins
*Le Bonhomme* (16 mm) 3 mins
*Episode de la vie de Monsieur Bonhomme* (animation) (16 mm) 3 mins
*Monsieur Mon Général* (animation) (16 mm) 3 mins

### 1966

*Dessin animé bavard comme pas un* (animation) (16 mm) 4 mins
*Sept péchés capitaux et militaires* (animation) (16 mm) 3 mins
*Les Mots* (animation) (16 mm) 2'30 mins
*Pierre Petit, mon ami* (16 mm) 20 mins

*Les Voleurs de Lune* (16mm) 18 mins

## 1967

*Au-delà de l'horizon* (animation) (16 mm) 13 mins
*Chantebredouille* (animation) (16 mm) 4 mins

## 1968

*Autoportrait* (16 mm) 8 mins

## 1969

*L'Espace vitale* (16 mm) 25 mins
*La Tiare d'Almendros* (final examination piece at the IDHEC) (16 mm) 25
   mins

## 1970

*Tout à la plume, rien au pinceau (and my name is Marcel Gotlib)* (16 mm) 30
   mins

## 1971

*Le Laboratoire de l'angoisse* (35 mm) 8 mins

## 1972/73

*La Famille heureuse (Famille Gazul)* (16 mm) 12 mins

## 1973

*Le Batteur de Boléro* (16 mm) 8'30 mins


## Feature films

### *Les Vécés étaient fermés de l'intérieur* (1975), 80 mins

Screenplay: Marcel Gotlib, Patrice Leconte
Direction: Patrice Leconte
Photography: Bruno Nuytten
Editing: Catherine Michel
Artistic direction: Jacques D'Ovidio
Sound: Alain Sempé
Music: Paul Misraki
Cast: Jean Rochefort (Pichard), Coluche (Charbonnier), Roland Dubillard
   (Gazul), Danielle Évenou (Gwendoline)
Production: Gaumont/ Alain Poiré

### Les Bronzés (1978), 90 mins

Screenplay: Patrice Leconte and the *Splendid* group (adapted from their play *Amours, Coquillages et crustacés* )
Direction: Patrice Leconte
Photography: Jean-François Robin
Editing: Noëlle Boisson
Artistic direction: Jacques D'Ovidio
Sound: Paul Lainé
Music: Alain Bernholc, Serge Gainsbourg
Cast: Josiane Balasko (Nathalie), Michel Blanc (Jean-Claude), Marie-Anne Chazel (Gigi), Chrsitian Clavier (Jérôme), Gérard Jugnot (Bernard), Thierry Lhermitte (Popeye), Dominique Lavanant (Christiane), Michel Creton (Bourseault), Luis Rego (Bobo), Martin Lamotte (Miguel), Bruno Moynot (l'homme au slip noir)
Production: Tinacra Films/Yves Rousset-Rouard

### Les Bronzés font du ski (1979), 90 mins

Screenplay: Patrice Leconte and the *Splendid* group
Direction: Patrice Leconte
Photography: Jean-François Robin
Editing: Noëlle Boisson
Artistic direction: Jacques D'Ovidio
Sound: Guillaume Sciama
Music: Pierre Bachelet
Cast: Josiane Balasko (Nathalie), Michel Blanc (Jean-Claude), Marie-Anne Chazel (Gigi), Christian Clavier (Jérôme), Gérard Jugnot (Bernard), Thierry Lhermitte (Popeye), Dominique Lavanant (Christiane), Maurice Chevit (Marius), Bruno Moynot (Météo)
Production: Tinacra Films/Yves Rousset-Rouard
Distribution: CCFC

### Viens chez moi, j'habite chez une copine (1980), 90 mins

Screenplay: Patrice Leconte and Michel Blanc (from a play by Luis Rego and Didier Kaminka)
Direction: Patrice Leconte
Photography: Bernard Zitzerman
Editing: Jacqueline Thiédot
Artistic direction: Ivan Maussion
Sound: Guillaume Sciama
Music: Renaud, Ramon Pipin and Jean-Philippe Goude
Cast: Bernard Giraudeau (Daniel), Michel Blanc (Guy), Thérèse Liotard (Françoise), Anémone (Adrienne), Christine Dejoux (Cécile), Marie-

Anne Chazel (Catherine)
Production: Christian Fechner/A2
Distribution: AMLF

### *Ma Femme s'appelle reviens* (1981), 85 mins

Screenplay: Patrice Leconte and Michel Blanc (adapted from *Singles*, an original script by Joseph Morhaim)
Direction: Patrice Leconte
Photography: Robert Fraisse
Editing: Jacqueline Thiédot
Artistic direction: Ivan Maussion
Sound: Bernard Rochut
Music: William Sheller
Cast: Michel Blanc (Bernard), Anémone (Nadine), Xavier Saint-Macary (Philippe), Catherine Gandois (Mireille), Pascale Rocard (Anne), Christophe Malavoy (Terry), Charlotte de Turkheim (patient), Patrick Bruel (François)
Production: Christian Fechner
Distribution: AMLF

### *Circulez, y'a rien à voir* (1983), 90 mins

Screenplay: Patrice Leconte and Martin Veyron
Direction: Patrice Leconte
Photography: Robert Fraisse
Editing: Joëlle Hache
Artistic direction: Éric Moulard
Sound: Alain Lachassagne
Music: Ramon Pipin and Jean-Philippe Goude
Cast: Jane Birkin (Hélène Duvernet), Michel Blanc (Leroux), Jacques Villeret (Pélissier), Michel Robbe (Marc), Luis Rego (Reska), Gaëlle Legrand (Martine), Martin Lamotte (the cook)
Production: Christian Fechner/A2
Distribution: AMLF

### *Les Spécialistes* (1984), 90 mins

Screenplay: Bruno Tardon adapted by Patrice Leconte, Patric Dewolf and Michel Blanc
Direction: Patrice Leconte
Photography: Eduardo Serra
Editing: Joëlle Hache
Artistic direction: Ivan Maussion, Jacques Bufnoir
Sound: Alain Lachassagne

Music: Éric Demarsan
Cast: Bernard Giraudeau (Paul Brandon), Gérard Lanvin (Stéphane Carella), Christiane Jean (Laura Durieux), Bertie Cortez (Gaetan Mazetti), Maurice Barrier (Kovacs), Jacques Nolot (policeman)
Production: Christian Fechner/A2
Distribution: Gaumont

### *Tandem* (1986), 91 mins

Screenplay: Patrice Leconte and Patrick Dewolf
Direction: Patrice Leconte
Photography: Denis Lenoir
Editing: Joëlle Hache
Artistic direction: Ivan Maussion
Sound: Alain Curvelier
Music: François Berheim
Cast: Jean Rochefort (Michel Mortez), Gérard Jugnot (Rivetot), Sylvie Granotier (bookseller), Julie Jézéquel (waitress), Jean-Claude Dreyfus (the adviser)
Production: Philippe Carcassonne and René Cleitman
Distribution: AMLF

### *Monsieur Hire* (1989), 81 mins

Screenplay: Patrice Leconte and Patrick Dewolf, adapted from Georges Simenon, *Les Fiançailles de Monsieur Hire*
Direction: Patrice Leconte
Photography: Denis Lenoir
Editing: Joëlle Hache
Artistic direction: Ivan Maussion
Sound: Pierre Lenoir
Music: Michael Nyman, Brahms
Cast: Michel Blanc (Monsieur Hire), Sandrine Bonnaire (Alice), Luc Thuillier (Émile), André Wilms (inspector)
Production: Philippe Carcassonne and René Cleitman
Distribution: UGC

### *Le Mari de la coiffeuse* (1990), 80 mins

Screenplay: Patrice Leconte and Claude Klotz
Direction: Patrice Leconte
Photography: Eduardo Serra
Editing: Joëlle Hache
Artistic direction: Ivan Maussion
Sound: Pierre Lenoir

Music: Michael Nyman

Cast: Jean Rochefort (Antoine), Anna Galiéna (Mathilde), Roland Bertin (Antoine's father), Maurice Chevit (Ambroise Dupré), Philippe Clévenot (Morvoisieux), Ticky Holgado (Morvoisieux's son-in-law), Michèle Laroque (adoptive mother)

Production: Lambart Prod./Thierry de Ganay

## *Tango* (1992), 88 mins

Screenplay: Patrice Leconte and Patrick Dewolf

Direction: Patrice Leconte

Photography: Eduardo Serra

Editing: Geneviève Winding

Artistic direction: Ivan Maussion

Sound: Pierre Lenoir

Music: Angélique and Jean-Claude Nachon

Cast: Philippe Noiret (François de Nemours (L'Élégant)), Richard Bohringer (Vincent Baraduc), Thierry Lhermitte (Paul), Miou-Miou (Marie), Judith Godrèche (Madeleine), Carole Bouquet (hotel guest), Jean Rochefort (her husband), Michèle Laroque (Vincent's wife)

Production: Cinéa, Hachette Première

Distribution: AMLF

## *Le Parfum d'Yvonne* (1993), 89 mins

Screenplay: Patrice Leconte adapted from the novel *Villa triste* by Patrick Modiano

Direction: Patrice Leconte

Photography: Eduardo Serra

Editing: Joëlle Hache

Artistic direction: Ivan Maussion

Sound: Paul Lainé

Music: Pascal Estève

Cast: Jean-Pierre Marielle (René Meinthe), Hippolyte Girardot (Victor), Sandra Majani (Yvonne), Richard Bohringer (Yvonne's uncle), Paul Guers (Daniel Hendrickx), Corinne Marchand (manageress of les Tilleuls)

Production: Lambart Prod./ Thierry de Ganay

## *Les Grands Ducs* (1995), 85 mins

Screenplay: Patrice Leconte and Serge Frydman

Direction: Patrice Leconte

Photography: Eduardo Serra

Editing: Joëlle Hache

Artistic direction: Ivan Maussion
Sound: Paul Lainé
Music: Angélique et Jean-Claude Nachon
Cast: Jean-Pierre Marielle (Georges Cox), Philippe Noiret (Victor Vialat), Jean Rochefort (Eddie Carpentier), Catherine Jacob (Carla Milo), Michel Blanc (Shapiron), Clotilde Courau (Juliette), Jacques Nolot (Marceau), Jacques Mathou (stage manager)
Production: Lambart Prod./ Thierry de Ganay
Distribution: Bac Films

### *Ridicule* (1996), 102 mins

Screenplay: Rémi Waterhouse, Michel Fessler, Eric Vicaut
Direction: Patrice Leconte
Photography: Thierry Arbogast
Editing: Joëlle Hache
Artistic direction: Ivan Maussion
Sound: Paul Lainé
Music: Antoine Duhamel
Cast: Charles Berling (Ponceludon de Malavoy), Jean Rochefort (Marquis de Bellegarde), Fanny Ardant (Comtesse de Blayac), Judith Godrèche (Mathilde de Bellegarde), Bernard Giraudeau (Abbé de Vilecourt), Bernard Dhéran (de Montaliéri), Maurice Chevit (lawyer), Jacques Mathou (Abbé de l'Épée), Albert Delpy (Baron de Guéret), Lucien Pascal (Monsieur de Blayac), Carlo Brandt (Chevalier de Milletail)
Production: Philippe Carcassonne, Cinéa, Epithéte

### *Une chance sur deux* (1998), 109 mins

Screenplay: Patrice Leconte, Patrick Dewolf, Serge Frydman
Direction: Patrice Leconte
Photography: Steven Poster
Editing: Joëlle Hache
Artistic direction: Ivan Maussion
Sound: Paul Lainé
Music: Alexandre Desplat
Cast: Alain Delon (Julien Vignal), Jean-Paul Belmondo (Léo Brassac), Vanessa Paradis (Alice Tomaso), Eric Defosse (Carella), Michel Aumont (Ledoyen), Alexandre Iakovlev (l'imper), Valéry Gataev (Anatoli Sharkov)
Production: Christian Fechner
Distribution: UFD

### La Fille sur le pont (1999), 90 mins

Screenplay: Serge Frydman
Direction: Patrice Leconte
Photography (b/w): Jean-Marie Dreujou
Editing: Joëlle Hache
Artistic direction: Ivan Maussion
Sound: Paul Lainé
Cast: Vanessa Paradis (Adèle), Daniel Auteuil (Gabor), Claude Aufaure
    (suicidal man), Bertie Cortez (Kusak), Nivola Donato (Monsieur Loyal),
    Demetre Georgalas (Takis), Catherine Lascault (Irène), Luc Palun
    (impressario), Isabelle Petit-Jacques (the bride), Frédéric Pfluger
    (contortionist)
Production: Christian Fechner
Distribution: UFD

### La Veuve de Saint-Pierre (2000), 110 mins

Screenplay: Claude Feraldo, adapted by Patrice Leconte
Direction: Patrice Leconte
Photography: Eduardo Serra
Editing: Joëlle Hache
Artistic direction: Ivan Maussion
Sound: Paul Lainé
Music: Pascal Estève
Cast: Juliette Binoche (Madame La), Daniel Auteuil (the Captain), Emir
    Kusturica (Neel Auguste), Michel Duchaussoy (the Governor), Catherine
    Lascault (la Malvilain), Ghyslain Tremblay (Chevassus), Marc Béland
    (Loïc), Reynald Bouchard (Louis Ollivier)
Production: Gilles Legrand, Frédérique Brillion
Distribution: Pathé

### Félix et Lola (2001), 89 mins

Screenplay: Patrice Leconte and Claude Klotz
Direction: Patrice Leconte
Photography: Jean-Marie Dreujou
Editing: Joëlle Hache
Artistic direction: Ivan Maussion
Sound: Paul Lainé
Music: Alain Bashung and Natacha Atlas
Cast: Philippe Torreton (Félix), Charlotte Gainsbourg (Lola), Alain
    Bashung (the man in black), Philippe du Janerand (the man in grey),
    Ahmed Guedayia (Karim), Philippe Soutan (Ludo), Muriel Combeau
    (Arlette), Didier Cauchy (Max), Emmanuelle Bataille (Marina),

Charlotte Maury-Sentier (Madame Lulu), Michel Such (Frantz), René Remblier (Albert), Nadia Barentin (Madame Irzou)
Production: Philippe Carcassonne

### Rue des plaisirs (2001), 95 mins

Screenplay: Serge Frydman
Direction: Patrice Leconte
Photography: Eduardo Serra
Editing: Joëlle Hache
Artistic direction: Ivan Maussion
Sound: Paul Lainé
Cast: Lætitia Casta (Marion), Patrick Timsit (Petit Louis), Vincent Elbaz (Dimitri Josco), Catherine Mouchet (Lena), Isabelle Spade (Camille), Bérangère Allaux (Violette)
Production: Philippe Carcassonne (Ciné b)

### L'Homme du train (2002), 87 mins

Screenplay: Claude Klotz
Direction: Patrice Leconte
Photography: Jean-Marie Dreujou
Editing: Joëlle Hache
Artistic direction: Ivan Maussion
Sound: Paul Lainé, Jean Goudier and Dominique Hennequin
Music: Pascale Estève
Cast: Jean Rochefort (Manesquier), Johnny Halliday (Milan), Jean-François Stévenin (Luigi), Charlie Nelson (Max), Pascal Parmentier (Sadko), Isabelle Petit-Jacques (Viviane), Edith Scob (Manesquier's sister), Maurice Chevit (hairdresser), Véronique Kapoyan (baker)
Production: Philippe Carcassonne

## Collaborative films

### Contre l'oubli (1991)

Text: Guy Bedos
Direction: Chantal Ackerman, René Allio, Denis Amar, Jean Becker, Jane Birkin, Bertrand Blier, Jean-Michel Carré, Alain Corneau, Constantin Costa-Gravas, Dominique Dante, Claire Denis, Raymond Depardon, Jacques Deray, Michel Deville, Jacques Doillon, Martine Franck, Gérard Frot-Coutaz, Bernard Giraudeau, Francis Girod, Jean-Luc Godard, Romain Goupil, Jean-Loup Hubert, Robert Kramer, Patrice Leconte, Sarah Moon, Michel Piccoli, Alain Resnais, Coline Serreau, Bertrand

Tavernier, Nadine Trintignant
Photography: Denis Lenoir
Production: Cinétévé

### *Lumière et compagnie* (1995)

Operating the camera of the Lumière brothers: Philippe Poulet, Didier Ferry
Direction: Merzak Allouache, Theo Angelopoulos, Vicente Aranda, Gabriel Axel, J.J.Bigas Luna, John Boorman, Youssef Chahine, Alain Corneau, Constantin Costa-Gravas, Raymond Depardon, Francis Girod, Peter Greenaway, Lasse Hallström, Michael Haneke, Hugh Hudson, James Ivory, Gaston Kabore, Abbas Kiarostami, Cédric Klapiche, Andrei Koncha-lovsky, Patrice Leconte, Spike Lee, Claude Lelouch, David Lynch, Ismail Merchant, Claude Miller, Idrissa Ouedraogo, Arthur Penn, Lucian Pintilie, Jacques Rivette, Helma Sanders-Brahms, Jerry Schatzberg, Nadine Trintignant, Fernando Trueba, Liv Ullman, Jaco van Dormel, Régis Wargnier, Wim Wenders, Yoshishige Yoshida, Yimou Zhang,
Photography: Sarah Moon
Editing: Roger Ikhlef and Timothy Miller
Sound: Bernard Rochut and Jean Casanova
Music: Jean-Jacques Lemêtre
Production: Cinétévé, La 7 Arte, Canal +

## Television

### *Toi si je voulais* (1988)

(episode of the series *Sueurs froides*)
Screenplay: Patrice Leconte (adapted from a novel by Louis C. Thomas)
Photography: Denis Lenoir
Editing: Dominique Auvray
Sound: Alain Curvelier
Cast: Gérard Jugnot (Philippe), Julie Jézéquel (Thérèse), Claude Chabrol (narrator)
Production: Christian Fechner/A2/Canal +

### *La Maladie orpheline* (1998)

Special documentary report directed by Patrice Leconte
Photography: Roger Motte
Editing: Emmanuel Maquaire
Sound: Richard Hayon
Production: A2

# Select bibliography

For interviews with the director, newspaper articles and film reviews, see the references section at the end of each chapter.

## Works by Leconte

*Je suis un imposteur*, Paris, Flammarion, 2000. An autobiographical account which treats the director's life and works via a series of anecdotal reflections on his apprenticeship and cinematic career, the making of his films, and his collaborations with directors, actors, writers and technical teams.

## Full-length works about Leconte

Chantier, Pascal and Lemeunier, Jean-Charles, *Patrice, Leconte et les autres*, Paris, Séguier, 2001. Taking as its pivot the heterogeneity of Leconte's *œuvre*, the book is presented in the form of a collection of fragments of text and image. It includes interviews with Leconte, his principal stars (including Lhermitte, Jugnot, Paradis and Auteuil), and his technical teams. Focusing on continuity as well as disparity, the authors identify some of the recurrent themes that haunt Leconte's cinema (masculinity, the couple, sexuality, failure, travel) and offer brief commentary on the formal and technical qualities that unite this body of films.

## Academic articles and book chapters

Downing, Lisa, 'Between Men and Women; Beyond Heterosexuality: Limits and Possibilities of the Erotic in Lynne Stopkewich's *Kissed* and Patrice Leconte's *La Fille sur le pont*', *Romance Studies* 20: 1, June 2002, 29–40. The article pursues a Butlerian reading (which contends that gender and sexuality function as modes of performative imitation for which there is no original) in order to explore the unusual portrayal of sexual desire in two films of the 1990s. It reads Leconte's film against the established critical grain as a self-aware text that problematizes discourses surrounding male–female desire, gesturing towards a queering of heterosexuality.

Downing, Lisa, review of Pascal Chantier and Jean-Charles Lemeunier, *Patrice, Leconte et les autres*, *Modern and Contemporary France* 11: 2, May 2003, 217–18.

Duffy, Jean H., 'Message Versus Mystery and Film Noir Borrowings in Patrice Leconte's *Monsieur Hire*', *French Cultural Studies* 13: 2: 38, 2002, 209–24. A thorough and insightful account of the extent to which *Monsieur Hire* both draws on and deviates from the conventions of the *film noir* genre. The article also undertakes meticulous close readings of some of the differences between Duvivier's *Panique* and Leconte's adaptation of the same novel: Simenon's *Les Fiançailles de Monsieur Hire*.

Murray, Abigail, 'Voyeurism in *Monsieur Hire*', *Modern and Contemporary France*, 3, July 1993, 287–95. The theme of voyeurism in *Monsieur Hire* is analysed in order to demonstrate that the mechanisms of gendered power-play at work in this filmic narrative are more complex and problematic than Laura Mulvey's canonical theoretical text on visual pleasure and narrative cinema would suggest.

Rosello, Mireille, 'Dissident Voices Before the Revolution: *Ridicule* (Leconte, 1996)' in Phil Powrie (ed.), *French Cinema in the 1990s: Continuity and Difference*, Oxford, Oxford University Press, 1999, 81–91. Rosello primarily examines *Ridicule* as a heritage film, evaluating the importance of the question of historical accuracy and exploring the extent to which Leconte uses a version of the past to reflect upon social questions of import in the present. Some theoretical reflection, using the thought of Michel Foucault and Judith Butler, is also brought to bear on the function of language in this film.

Sutton, Paul, '*Afterwardsness* in Film: Patrice Leconte's *Le Mari de la coiffeuse*', *French Studies*, 53: 3, July 1999, 307–17. A subtle psychoanalytic reading of the structure of this filmic narrative, which maps Freud's theories of melancholia and *Nachträglichkeit* (deferral or 'afterwardsness') on to cinematic devices such as the flashback. The article contains a

good deal of technical language and may be challenging for readers
unfamiliar with psychoanalytic thought.

Vanderschelden, Isabelle, 'Subtitling Wit: The Case of *Ridicule*', *Studies in
French Cinema*, 2: 2, 2002, 109–22. The Anglo-American and French
receptions of *Ridicule* are compared and contrasted. It is proposed that
*Ridicule* serves the function for non-French viewers of exemplifying a
specifically French type of intellectualism. Given the importance attributed to the subtle use of language in the film, some of the problems
inherent in the subtitling of *Ridicule* for an English market are put
under scrutiny.

# Index

Note: 'n.' after a page reference indicates the number of a footnote found on that page.